Peace Can Be Won

Peace Can Be Won

Paul G. Hoffman

Doubleday & Company, Inc., Garden City, N.Y., 1951

To Arthur H. Vandenberg, Senior Senator from
Michigan, whose words and works for peace
will always be an inspiration to those who
love peace.

Acknowledgment

I am listed as the author of this book. But I have had so much help from my associates in ECA in writing it that, in a sense, ECA should be listed rather than I.

I am particularly grateful to Hart Preston and Herbert Harris, who have worked with me very closely.

I should make it clear that I am solely responsible for the program which is recommended.

P.G.H.

Contents

Peace Can Be Won

In Peace or War, Our Aim Is Peace

In my Washington apartment one evening late last spring Bernard Baruch was our guest for dinner. The conversation turned to a speech I was planning to give at Wellesley College. In this speech, as I explained to Mr. Baruch, I was hoping to make clear to the Wellesley students and alumnae something of the nature of the titanic struggle taking place between our free world and the Kremlin.

Our guest has been long recognized as an authority on this crucial topic of our times, and as we discussed it he leaned forward eagerly, tilting his hearing aid first toward Mrs. Hoffman and then toward me.

When I told Mr. Baruch that the title of my talk was to be "The Cold War Is a Good War," his reply was characteristically abrupt. "You'll never make people understand the true character of this fight," he said, "until you stop talking about the 'cold war' and start talking about waging the peace."

I followed Mr. Baruch's advice and I did talk at Wellesley about waging the peace. A few days later, events like seismic shocks went sweeping round the world. On the surface it seemed that to be preoccupied with peace was to be unrealistic. On June 25, 1950, the North Koreans launched their aggression against the Republic of Korea. In usual Communist double talk they described it as a "peace march," even as their tanks and artillery swarmed across the 38th Parallel. The Security Council of the United Nations labeled the attack an unprovoked invasion and called "upon all members to render every assistance to stop aggression." The forces of the United Nations which responded to that call, forces which came largely from the United States, have met with fluctuating fortunes, disasters and triumphs. International tensions rose toward climax as the North Korean Army was reinforced by several hundred thousand new troops—the Chinese "volunteers."

The world situation had become so threatening that on December 16, 1950, President Truman proclaimed a state of national emergency. Barely six years after V-J Day, we in America are partially mobilizing our men, our materials and our machines, fusing them into military might. In the meantime, the Kremlin is looking with ever more naked avidity upon the oil fields of Iran and Saudi Arabia. And inside almost every other country, not only in France and Italy, but in Lebanon, Brazil and Indonesia, Communist agitation, subversion, propaganda and sabotage are increasing in speed and scope. Like a thunderhead over western Europe is the menace of a Red Army march to the Atlantic.

I well know that all these moves and movements mean that the free world was never in greater peril. For that very reason I believe that we must concern ourselves with peace as never before. Nor do I believe that a concern with peace today is an indulgence in wishful thinking.

I suggest that the exact opposite is true. To be sure, we may be forced to fight a third world war despite the efforts of the United Nations and our own statesmen. In that event we must enter it with a clearly defined program for peace which will give a sound direction to the conduct of that war. We should wage war not to win a war, but to win a peace.

I contend that we still have the opportunity to avoid a general war if we begin at once to wage the peace with imagination, boldness and a sense of dedication. Otherwise we deny our instincts as a peace-hungry people; otherwise we forfeit our obligation as reasonably sane and civilized human beings to prevent a holocaust more dreadful than any ever known.

To wage the peace intelligently we must realize the kind of war that threatens us. The Soviet Union has been and is carrying on a completely new kind of war against the non-Communist world, as such astute analysts as Rear Admiral Bern Anderson (U.S.N., Ret.) are pointing out. To most of us the very word war calls up images of blood and havoc, of physical violence and destruction, of armies clashing, roads choked with refugees, the rubble of cities and of oil slicks on the seas. To most of us war's aim and end is victory on the field. But to the Kremlin military action is but the most visible and spectacular zone of combat in an unremitting war against the free world. Herein lies our strange and new and often hidden danger—a danger that we cannot fend off by arms alone. We must know that for the Kremlin the military is only one of four fronts—each a battleground of implacable attack. These four fronts are the military, economic, political and psychological. Lenin himself has defined them. He has declared that they comprise the four interlocking parts of a "most determined and ruthless war, a persistent struggle, bloody and bloodless, violent and peaceful, military and economic, educational and administrative—against the forces and traditions of the old society."

Along the military front, the Soviet Union has, as we know, mobilized and equipped a gigantic war machine of its own and commandeered within its camp the military potential of its satellites in eastern Europe and its partners and puppets in Asia.

Along the economic front, the Soviet Union has geared to a war economy its own farms and factories and those of all nations within its orbit. In areas outside of its direct control it has sought to derange and to damage economic stability and progress. It foments strikes, sabotage and slowdowns. It exploits the worker's discontent with his low wage, the peasant's resentment against high rent for his land when he has it and his hunger for land when he has none.

On the political front, the Soviet Union has denied free vote and voice to its own people and all those whom it has enslaved. In free countries, its agents scatter among the peoples the seeds of doubt in the honesty, motives and workings of their governments. It attempts to set nation against nation, to wreck alliances and allegiances within the free world, and to use its membership in the United Nations to thwart every effort toward international co-operation.

On the psychological front, the Soviet Union breeds strife, suspicion and distrust among all strata of society, turning the employee against the employer, the middle class against the peasant and all against each other. It magnifies minor political and economic differences into major discords. Its working capital is insecurity; its chief investment is in the manufacture of hate. It uses the poverty it has helped to engender and prolong to whet appetite for its own false claims to plenty.

This is the nature of the new kind of war that the Union of Soviet Socialist Republics has declared against the United States and the entire free world. It is waging that war along all four fronts to gain its goal of world conquest. To defeat this purpose, we must wage the peace along the same four fronts—the military, the economic, the political and the psychological.

In this venture we well know that different aims require different methods. The Kremlin wants to divide, conquer and enslave. Hence it inevitably uses totalitarian techniques of coercion, violence and terror. We want to unite peoples, co-operate with them, help them to gain and keep freedom. Hence we inevitably will continue to use our own democratic tools of free choice, open debate and voluntary decision.

In the days ahead every one of us must wage the peace. We must work for it and at it. Lest we lose what we are and all we seek to become, each one of us must stand and be counted among the legions of the free.

CHAPTER 2

To Win the Peace We Must Wage the Peace

In waging war we know that we cannot win by ignoring the brutal facts, by wringing our hands or by withholding the dollars needed for victory. On the contrary, we know that victory can result only from recruiting our best minds to develop brilliant and imaginative over-all strategy, from spending hundreds of billions of dollars to put that strategy into effect, from the dedication of our skills and energies to the task of winning. You remember during World War II how quickly many of our ablest citizens rushed to Washington to serve their country, how eagerly Congress appropriated—not billions, but tens of billions—for war purposes, how we rolled up our sleeves and built guns, tanks, planes and ships, worked in Red Cross and sold war bonds.

War? That is easy to grasp. Fighting is violent and

spectacular, something you can feel and see, something you can support.

Peace? Peace is quiet and dull and intangible. It doesn't make headlines, yet we can make it dramatic and tangible—if we work at it. It has been our failure to understand that we must work at it day in and day out that accounts for the disasters which plagued us in the wake of our Civil War and our participation in World Wars I and II.

If, after the Civil War, the North had accepted Lincoln's precept of "malice toward none; with charity for all" and waged the peace by promoting recovery in the South, it could quickly have restored good will, understanding and prosperity. A few million dollars loaned to the Southern states to help them acquire feed and livestock and plows for farms and plantations would have added hundreds of millions to the wealth of the nation. With such assistance the South could have staged a faster comeback in ten years than it did in thirty. The United States could thus have become reunited, in a real sense, almost overnight. But instead of economic aid the North sent carpetbaggers. And more than fifty years after the Civil War had ended, I could personally testify as a Northern recruit in a Southern camp, to the resentment and bitterness that were the result of the North's blindness in not waging the peace.

In the immediate period after World War I we might

also have won the peace if we had worked at it with vigor and imagination. From Stockholm to Seattle to Samarkand, the people wanted peace. But we didn't work at it. Instead, we in the United States spurned the League of Nations. We returned to the "normalcy" of our isolationism. Great Britain and France reverted to the normalcy of that mutual distrust which gave Hitler the green light to build his war machine.

It would not be fair to say we didn't work at waging peace, at least to some extent, after World War II. During the past three years especially, what with the Truman Doctrine, the Marshall Plan, the North Atlantic Treaty Organization (NATO), the Mutual Defense Assistance Program and our eagerness to make the UN effective, we have been reaching out for peace with ever-greater awareness. But so far we have failed, and mainly for two reasons. First of all, it took most of us too long to perceive that the masters of the Kremlin have decided that it is the manifest destiny of the Soviet state to dominate the earth. The Kremlin has made adroit use of our unwillingness, even our refusal, to face this rough-edged reality. After V-J Day we indulged in an orgy of escapism. We busied ourselves in rushing the boys home from Europe—exactly what the Kremlin wanted. We tooled up to turn out television sets. But during this same period the USSR had tooled up to fling the world's most intricate radar screen against the sky. And while we

21

concerned ourselves with "business as usual," the USSR was breeding plans for aggression and aggrandizement that had been long and meticulously prepared. Under the giant shadow of the Red Army, such states as Poland, Hungary, Rumania and Bulgaria were swiftly shackled to the USSR.

Communist traitors took over Czechoslovakia by internal coup. And to soften up other free nations as preface to Soviet control, Moscow commanded hard-core Communist cells in trade unions and universities, in journalism and in agriculture, to intensify their efforts to sabotage production, to sap faith in orderly democratic government and to spread the Big Lie. And in China, Mao Tse-tung, with T-square and compass made in Moscow, was drawing up the final blueprint for Communist control of the Far East.

The second reason we failed to attain a secure peace after World War II lay in our inability to grasp the magnitude of the program this required. To be sure, we took the vital first step by helping to organize the United Nations. We displayed an openhanded generosity toward the rest of the world. We mailed millions of pounds of food and clothing parcels to Europeans in distress. Our government loaned Britain $3,750,000,000 just a year after V-E Day. We funneled more than $2,500,000,000 into the United Nations Relief and Rehabilitation Administration (UNRRA). We gave Europe more than $555,000,000 through the Interim Aid Program. We spent millions in China. We backed the International Bank for Reconstruction and Development. All in all, even before ECA, we extended some $12,000,000,000 in aid to Europe alone. Unfortunately, our aid lost much of its effectiveness because it was administered on a stopgap, emergency basis without a comprehensive plan. It could not do enough to fend off the chaos contrived by the Kremlin.

But how, then, should the peace be waged? Opinions on this score naturally reflect every gradation, but two extreme views stand out. A dwindling group of Americans still believe that we can reconcile our differences with the USSR by adjusting them over the council table. This approach represents the well-known "we-can-do-business-with-Stalin" school. At the opposite end is the growing group of Americans who believe that, since the USSR is inevitably going to attack us, we should get the jump on it by starting war first. This approach represents the even better known "preventive-war" school.

Both attitudes merit examination.

For some time after the end of World War II, I felt that the Kremlin, if frustrated in its campaign to take over Western Europe by internal coups such as the one engineered in Czechoslovakia, might shift its sights from world dominion to the task of improving the lot of the Soviet people. The USSR was then, and is now, spending at least 35 per cent of its gross national income in building armed forces either for foreign war or to suppress internal opposition. Clearly, if Russia turned away from this war economy it could divert at least two-thirds of its outlays on armies and navies to lift living standards from Leningrad to Vladivostok. It seemed to me that this made good sense and that the Kremlin might think so too. It was my hope, in short, that the Kremlin would decide to live and let live.

In this respect, in common with most Americans, I made a grievous miscalculation that may do credit to our spirit of tolerance but hardly to our sense of *Realpolitik*. Despite the Kremlin's attempt to justify seizure of eastern European countries as a rough-handed security measure, a need to forge a ring of buffer states between the USSR and potential foes, it is now clear that her moves in this area, as in all others, are only station stops on her timetable of world conquest.

The Kremlin's intent, even before the Marshall Plan got under way, became abundantly clear as early as July 1947 in Paris. General Marshall had but recently delivered his great speech at Harvard, calling upon the nations of Europe, upon all of them, to join together in a vast co-operative effort to repair their shattered economies. "It is logical," he had declared, "that the United States should do *whatever it is able to do to assist* in the return of normal economic health in the world, without which there can be no political stability and no assured peace. Our policy is directed not against any country or doctrine, but against hunger, poverty, desperation and chaos." There were no ideological strings attached to that offer beyond the common-sense warning that "governments, political parties or groups which seek to perpetuate human misery in order to profit therefrom politically or otherwise will encounter the opposition of the United States." This was an offer made in good faith and backed by good will. Its sole object was to lay the groundwork for a more prosperous world in which peace and freedom would be secure.

Electrified by the implications of this offer, British Foreign Secretary Ernest Bevin had within a matter of hours called Georges Bidault, the French Foreign Minister. Together they promptly asked V. M. Molotov, the USSR's Foreign Minister, to meet them for discussions. Ten days later the three sat down around the oval table in the cream-and-gilt conference room of the Quai d'Orsay. For a short hopeful time it appeared that something close to co-operative action on the part of all Europe was about to emerge. Then, on the sixth day, Molotov walked out with neither explanation nor goodbys and enplaned for Moscow. The satellite governments of Poland, Hungary, Bulgaria, Rumania, Albania and Yugoslavia, upon orders from Moscow, refused invitations to the general Europe-wide conference that soon followed. Similarly, Czechoslovakia, at the last moment, was "persuaded" by the Kremlin to withdraw from any Marshall Plan explorations.

Molotov's departure was not merely another churlish Russian gesture. It was, in fact, the USSR's declaration of the "cold war." It reflected the Politburo's decision that the USSR, to continue to exist under its present rulers, not only had to oppose recovery in the free world but also had to destroy the free world. As the vanguard vehicle to accomplish this dual objective, the Cominform was set up under the auspices of the Soviet Union in September 1947, to defeat the Marshall Plan as the instrument of "United States imperialism." In the three years that have elapsed since the onset of the Marshall Plan the Soviet Union has reached new depths of conscious duplicity to cancel out all our efforts to promote recovery in the free world. It has nullified agreements. It has violated treaties. It has double-crossed us and the rest of the free world time and time again.

I personally recall that the Kremlin, in its recent dealings with the United States, has broken these major promises:

1. At the Teheran Conference of 1943 the Soviet Union pledged that Poland and all other nations, later engorged as satellites, would have "the right of all peoples to choose the form of government under which they wish to live." In not one case has this right been granted.

2. The Soviet Union at the Potsdam Conference of 1945 pledged that all democratic political parties throughout Germany should be encouraged. But only the Communist-run Socialist Unity party obtained Soviet support in the Russian zone, and all other political factions were either suppressed or their independence ruthlessly rooted out.

3. At Potsdam the Soviet Union agreed that Japanese soldiers, once disarmed, would be allowed to return to their homes "with an opportunity to lead peaceful and productive lives." Of 377,000 Japanese prisoners, only 95,000 have been returned.

4. On June 7, 1945, the four great powers—the United States, United Kingdom, China and Soviet Russia—agreed not to use willfully their veto power to obstruct the functioning of the UN Security Council. The number of Soviet vetoes since then has reached the not inconsiderable total of forty-seven.

5. After its moral defeat by the Berlin airlift, the Soviet Union agreed in Paris on June 20, 1949, that each occupying power in Germany would "insure the normal functioning" of all transport between the Western and Russian zones. But early in 1950 the Soviet commandant was intermittently stopping traffic and hampering all trade and communication between the Eastern and Western zones.

6. The Soviet Union also agreed that Korea, "in due

course," would become free and independent. It refused, however, to allow a United Nations commission to enter or investigate conditions in the Korean territory north of the 38th Parallel.

Since Soviet behavior in Korea merely spells out again its essential pattern of conquest, as already applied to the European scene, it would seem useless to try to do business with Stalin. His price is too high. He wants us, among other things, to cease rearming Western Europe, to put Eastern Germany completely under Soviet sway, to share supervision of Western Germany with the USSR, to give Southeast Asia over to the Soviet Union and Communist China by withdrawing the Seventh Fleet from Formosa and our armed forces from Korea and from the South Pacific generally. Stalin means to have a decisive voice in shaping Japan's future and to transfer the UN seat now occupied by the Chinese Nationalists to the Mao regime. Stalin wants, above all, to isolate the United States in a Communist sea where, as the last island of freedom, it could be washed away by the relentless pounding of Communist tides.

Someday when the free world has demonstrated to Stalin and his liege men at home and abroad that it is so strong, so resolute, so unified that he cannot undermine it, negotiations might yield fruit. But not now, not now for a while.

What, then, about waging a preventive war? The

proponents of such a course argue very plausibly. "Let's drop the bomb now," they say. "The Communist attack on Korea made absolutely clear the Kremlin's warlike and aggressive intentions. Why should we sit righteously on our hands and let the Russians pick their own time and place for a new Pearl Harbor?"

I can understand why many people feel this way. Much as I believe in peace, I am not for peace at any price. I go along completely with Senator Vandenberg, who, with his customary insight, said at Dartmouth College in 1949: "Appeasement is surrender on the installment plan." And General Marshall, in his eloquent 1950 Memorial Day address, endorsed this view when he declared that "there is nothing to be said in favor of war except that it is the lesser of two evils. For it *is* better than appeasement of aggression because appeasement encourages the very aggression it seeks to prevent."

Yet today I do not believe that we are faced by a dilemma so direful that we have no choice but to cast mankind into the darkness of global war. I believe that an attempt to crush Communism with atomic bombs would be to miss the objective, like the bull that charges the cape instead of the matador. To wage a preventive war against the Kremlin would be to substitute emotion for intelligence, panic for resourcefulness. You do not prevent a war by starting one.

The late Wendell Willkie flew around the world in the summer of 1942 and came back talking about America's "reservoir of good will." That good will, he had discovered, was based on a concept abroad of the United States as a generous and non-aggressive nation. He found that, although our early defeats in World War II had cost us a few "friends" who decided to play the apparent winners, the majority of the world's peoples not only admired our moral position in holding our fire until attacked but actually wanted to help us. Since Willkie's "one-world" journey America has finished a global war, helped to re-establish order and helped other nations to help themselves. The Kremlin has filled the air with charges that we are imperialists and warmongers. But a vast portion of the world still looks to America as the symbol of peace with freedom and its best ally against aggression. For the United States now to launch an aggression—no matter how justified it might appear to be—would be to impair our moral stature. It would be an admission that we lacked the brain power and the will power to wage the peace so boldly and effectively on the four fronts of the military (in terms of making the free world's defenses impregnable), the political, the economic and the psychological, that out of desperation we had to be the first to resort to force.

Moreover, to begin a preventive war, no matter the provocation, is an act of aggression; and if aggression is morally wrong for everybody else, it is also morally wrong for us. We cannot afford a double standard of morality in peace or in war. Our moral standing is among our most valuable assets. I also believe that we can retain our own moral self-respect only so long as what we do can be approved by our own conscience and that of mankind.

Let us assume, however, that the preventive war doctrine should win out in the planning councils. Some night, at a dozen secret bases, B-36 bombers would load up with atom bombs and roar off into the darkness. Their targets would be Moscow, Leningrad, the steelworks at Magnitogorsk, and the cyclotrons at "Atomgrad," and other industrial centers. Would they get there and successfully destroy Russia's ability to wage war? This is not a question that I—or probably anyone—can answer accurately, especially since many Soviet plants producing war matériel have been placed underground. But there is no question that the Russians have enough of a radar ring and sufficient interceptors and anti-aircraft batteries to make the venture a hazardous gamble.

Even if we did ruin many of Russia's cities and destroy some of its factories, it would still be able to carry on the fight with its great land army of some 175 divisions. Facing them across the border in Western Europe at present would be a small force in Germany of

American, British, and French troops and a handful of NATO divisions in France, Italy, Belgium, Norway, Denmark and Holland. They could not effectively oppose Soviet armies, and much of free Europe would soon be overrun. We would be faced with the job of liberating the whole continent. Once again we would find ourselves bombing our friends as well as our enemies and once again—if we were to drive the invaders out of Europe—we would face another D-Day and another blood bath on Normandy beaches. How long it would take us to gain victory no one knows. I am sure that in time we could win. But I am also sure that it would be a long and hard and horrible struggle—exactly the opposite of the quick victory which the preventive war group proposes and expects.

That, for my money, is the kind of disaster likely to result from any hasty bomb dropping.

Furthermore, I strongly feel that any campaign waged in the United States in favor of preventive war can do us immeasurable harm abroad.

The western Europeans are joining us in full partnership to prevent the Soviet Union from waging aggressive war. But they would be unwilling to stand with us in starting an aggressive war against the Soviet Union even though this might be thoroughly justified. Even the talk of preventive war frightens Europeans. They are war-weary. They have lived through the agonies of two devastating wars waged on their own soil within a single generation, wars that caused even the grass to grow red, as the peasants say. They have but recently begun to emerge from ruins and to build again and to hope again. The prospect of having their lands once more turned into battlefields remains a "nightmare at noon." The courage summoned forth by Europe's free nations in combining to stop Soviet-inspired aggression might well falter if those same nations suspected that the United States, in its turn, was about to counter with aggression on its own.

Finally, bomb-dropping talk in the United States provides the Soviet Union with just the slogans its propaganda machine needs to maneuver us into the position of being the war party.

I agree with a recent column in the New York *Times,* in which military analyst Hanson Baldwin labeled the preventive war doctrine the "course of political bankruptcy and moral frustration that would be militarily ineffective and which would lose for the United States the very values we are trying to defend."

But if "we can't do business with Stalin" and if we are not to "drop the bomb," what then? My answer is a positive program that goes beyond mere containment. It calls for wresting the initiative from the USSR not only by anticipating its moves, and thus thwarting them, but even more importantly by eradicating the social and political and economic conditions on which Communism thrives. In this respect the Marshall Plan has been and remains pilot plant and proving ground for an American foreign policy that is firm, constructive and far-reaching. For the first time the Soviet Union's boring-from-within strategy has been halted and hurled back as the Marshall Plan's hydroelectric power plants and housing developments and tractors and seed have been set against Marxist dialectic; as the Marshall Plan's bread and butter are set in contrast to the hollow cake of the Big Lie.

Necessarily, in today's world, the kind of program I suggest must be buttressed by the creation of an armed defense force formidable enough to keep the Red Army from marching at the same time that we are keeping the Soviet Union off balance by vigorous offensives along the economic, political and psychological fronts.

I believe that this program offers a reasonable prospect for avoiding World War III, preserving the liberties of those peoples who still are governed by consent and laying the groundwork for peace with freedom.

By peace with freedom I mean a peace that is more than the absence of war and a freedom that is more than the absence of slavery.

It means, as I see it, that "life, liberty, and the pursuit of happiness" can become the living faith for all men.

CHAPTER 3

The United States:
Reluctant Leader of the Free World

I have the greatest confidence that we can wage the peace, and wage it successfully, if the United States accepts the responsibilities of world leadership. My entire program is based on the premise that only we have the material resources, the mastery of the industrial arts, the strategic position and the organizational drive to lead the fight for peace. Reluctant as we are to assume our new role in the world, we must play it well or assent to dark days of chaos as preface to the unending night of totalitarian enslavement.

But to take on leadership of the free world does not mean that we should, on the basis of our comparative strength, be expected to carry the whole load or even a disproportionate share of it. It is not in our nature to quibble over such *quid pro quos* in a narrow legalistic fashion. We know that it is only enlightened self-interest, which is common sense with a college degree, to buttress the security of other nations on our side. We can furnish them with troops and supplies and economic assistance. However, the acid test of our leadership will be our ability to inspire and inspirit them to carry with vigor and pride their own proportionate shares of the common defense burden.

I didn't find it easy to accept the reality that our own security is inseparably linked with that of other free nations. My father was born within a few blocks of the old Chicago *Tribune* office building at Dearborn and Madison. I was born and grew up in the Chicago area—hundreds of miles from either ocean and thousands of miles from Europe and Asia. By both instinct and indoctrination I was isolationist. But it took only the first of the two world wars to convince me that we in the United States could not turn our backs on the rest of the world and live alone, no matter how much we liked it. During the make-a-million twenties and the down-and-out thirties that followed I saw booms and depressions sweep across the globe with no regard for boundary lines. I saw the new totalitarianisms—Communism, Fascism, Nazism—grow into menacing might. I began to realize that there was no way we could insulate ourselves against the impact of these new world forces. But it remained for Walter Lippmann, in a series of prophetic lectures at the University of Chicago in 1938, to sharpen and crystallize my ideas of America's place in this new kind of interdependent world.

"In our time," argued Mr. Lippmann, "we shall witness the dawning realization that a new power exists which is destined to be a successor of Rome and of Britain as the giver of peace, and that its mission is to prepare itself for the accomplishment of that destiny. I refer, of course, to the United States of America." Looking back on it, I wonder if Lippmann knew how soon we would be called upon to play that part. I do remember that he offered some sound advice. "It is better to play the part knowingly rather than to drift," he said. "However much Americans today may dislike it, they cannot refuse it. Their greatness, their position and their power among the peoples of the earth imply that they must accept their destiny. They must accept the enormous burdens and the heavy responsibilities."

Of course America was not ready in 1938 to assume even a modest responsibility in international affairs. Instead, we were in a mood of wishful thinking. We were relying on our "neutrality acts" to keep us out of a world war if it should come. World War II did come, and after a vast amount of political fanfare with both presidential candidates in the 1940 election promising to keep our boys at home, we found millions of them abroad only four years later, slugging it out with the

Nazis and Fascists and Japanese on a dozen major fronts.

For most people, America's participation in two world wars is at least circumstantial evidence that the United States cannot stand aside, and alone, if chaos and destruction swirl about us. And some circumstantial evidence is very strong. If you are sitting on a fence and a bullet whizzes by—perhaps no conclusion can be drawn; if a *second* bullet takes a similar course, you are warranted in entertaining a suspicion that all is not well. However, if a third bullet puts a hole in your hat and parts your hair, you are justified in concluding that someone is out to get you.

There are, of course, a few people who, despite two world wars and much other "circumstantial" evidence, still hold that we can abandon Europe and Asia and do business as usual on our great island continent. They insist that we should keep all dollars at home and devote them to throwing up bastions that stop at our own borders. I doubt that any defense could be devised to offer us safety under such a program of "armed isolation" if Western Europe were to be overrun by the Soviet Union. I think that it would be majestic folly to try to build a Fortress America and let the rest of the world go by. A brief glimpse of our need for strategic materials obtainable only from beyond our own borders should dispel the illusions of those who look upon the Atlantic and Pacific oceans as protective moats. We have to import, for example, some ninety per cent of our manganese vital to steelmaking, most of our bauxite for aluminum, and all of our tin and natural rubber, to cite only a few commodities crucial to our kind of industrial society. But assume for the sake of argument that it would be possible to construct such isolationist ramparts. Then we would have to maintain them, not for months or years, but for decades. The cost of defense, even with Western Europe on our side, is already a prodigious burden. But, without Western Europe, the cost would be more staggering still.

In terms of present dollars that cost would amount to perhaps $125,000,000,000 a year for ourselves alone in contrast to our current expenditures of some $25,000,-000,000 for ourselves *and* our allies. And the worst of it is that the cost would grow, decade by decade, as the military strength of Kremlin-dominated Europe and Asia continued to expand. Unavoidably, our living standards would be pounded down toward spartan levels if such a disproportionate share of our resources were to be diverted to military purposes. Worst of all, and most frightening, is the prospect that this necessary diversion of resources could be accomplished only by invoking the full paraphernalia of the controls we associate with the totalitarian state—not, I repeat, for months or years, but for decades.

Here is a terrifying pitfall; for in creating this form of

39

self-sufficient defense, we place in jeopardy the very freedoms we are most eager to defend. It is one thing to give up a free economy for a short emergency period, but quite another to give it up for a long period. Even those far more optimistic than I (and I *am* an optimist) can hardly sustain the belief that a vast bureaucracy, long entrenched, would be too eager to give up the right to direct our personal and business lives once the peril was over. And with its influence over votes it could acquire a longevity that would be difficult, if not impossible, to oust.

Warning against the dangers of "armed isolation," the Hartford *Courant,* in an editorial published December 21, 1950, said:

Before the nation adopts this as a policy it should think it through to the end. If we do we shall find that it can mean nothing else than making of the United States an armed and frightened and regimented camp. Our coming $100,-000,000,000 budgets would be pin money compared to what would be required to survive in such solitude. Today's tense jitteriness would be the normal order of life. The tough but temporary controls we now need would be permanent. We would stand all alone. And we would be at the mercy of the first trigger-happy Communist to let loose the first atom bomb.

Almost all of us have now reluctantly accepted America's new position of leadership in the world. But this does not automatically signify that we understand how that leadership can best affirm itself in ideas and action which reflect the national will and the national character. If we are to lead effectively *we must work with the rest of the free world on a basis of partnership and unity,* founded on respect for views and interests other than our own. This is a matter of elementary psychology—an operating principle just as valid for heads of state as for the men in the street. The men who determine the policies of the other free nations are, without exception, eager to work with us; almost without exception, they would resent dictation from us. I learned this well during my time as ECA administrator.

Soon after I resigned from this post I made on ECA's behalf an inspection tour of European recovery in October 1950. I found that the best results invariably appeared where we had done the most to achieve joint understanding. Turkey is an excellent example.

Our enemy in World War I, a neutral in World War II, Turkey has now become one of our most dependable partners. The basis for US-Turkish friendship is, of course, mutual self-interest. But the friendship has been greatly advanced by mutual respect. At the Turkish "White House" I talked with Turkey's President Celal Bayar. Between sips of sweet wine and black coffee he told me how eager Turkey was to share in building up the defenses of the free world. Turkey is doing just that; a nation of twenty million, it maintains a well-disciplined standing army of twenty-two to twenty-five divisions, along with universal military training. Moreover, Turkey, sharing a frontier with a Russia that urgently wants control of the strategic Dardanelles, has been consistently standing up to the Kremlin. Yet I shudder to think of the reaction of this proud and wise leader of the Turkish people if (as some "back-seat" drivers had often demanded) I had told him we would continue Marshall Plan aid only if his generals deployed a dozen divisions at a certain spot at a certain time. To be firm, even to be tough, does not mean to be dictatorial; we must always keep in mind that the essence of genuine leadership is to share power *with* people rather than display power *over* people.

In Great Britain, Ernest Bevin discussed with me the problems of leadership. Britain, of course, was the dominant world power from the time she defeated the Spanish Armada at the end of the sixteenth century until World War I. Bevin, who, despite his Socialism, has tremendous pride in the historical accomplishments of Empire, was trying to sift out the reasons why it had so long endured. "Some people contended," he said, "that our power rested on the gold braid and tassels of our admirals and ninety thousand sailors. But I say that the

Empire's strength lay in the respect that the world had for British fairness, British culture and our incorruptible system of courts and justice."

Britain was a great leader, and she earned her greatness. Her major contribution to the technique of leadership was to create that association of peoples first called the Empire and later the Commonwealth. Empire, of course, is a word repugnant to Americans. Yet an association of peoples who rule themselves and act for the common good is, we can hope, the pattern of the future. Just as Britain, within the Commonwealth, has become the first among equals, so the United States has the opportunity to become the first among equals of today's free world.

Hence, we must do all we can to energize those international organizations that are the guardians of the free world's strength. The United Nations is, of course, the major vehicle for our efforts toward unity in dealing with other peoples. We must support it unstintingly. We must also continue to support such regional organizations as the Council of Europe (the beginning of a European parliament), the Organization for European Economic Cooperation (which has worked with ECA to integrate Europe's economy), the North Atlantic Treaty Organization (the instrument of military co-ordination between North America and Europe) and the Pan American Union. As yet unratified by the United States

Congress is the International Trade Organization (a vehicle for expediting trade among all nations) which, on balance, I believe we should join. There are many provisions in the ITO charter which, because they encourage statism, I do not like; but I prefer an international trade organization with an imperfect charter to no international trade organization. As members working on the inside, we would have the right to press for the acceptance of our own ideas.

But neither governments nor their agencies have the sole responsibility of promoting unity among free peoples. Every individual can and must take personal part in the war against lies. Free peoples must begin to believe the best and not the worst of what they hear of each other if they are to work as partners.

More often than we realize, we engage in maligning other free nations or spreading propaganda about them. When we do, we give emphatic aid to Soviet attempts to turn us against each other. The Communist propaganda mill is daily planting rumors designed for fertile growth within the free nations. Take one recent month's grist: America was fed a fantasy that Great Britain is devoting much of her aircraft-engine capacity to building jet planes for Russia. France was fed the falsehood that America is secretly rearming millions of Germans, while rumors ricocheted through Germany that France will insist on dismantling the entire Ruhr and other industrial centers until Germany becomes an economic grave-yard.

Benjamin Franklin said it, but no other slogan is more suited to our time: "We must all hang together, or assuredly we shall all hang separately."

CHAPTER 4

The Penalty of Leadership

In 1915 the Cadillac Motor Company published an advertisement under the title "The Penalty of Leadership," which is still remembered in United States advertising circles. Leadership, it stressed, carries its penalties as well as its rewards. Leadership does impose great burdens. Every businessman knows that once his product and company achieve leadership the compulsion to maintain quality and to live up to the highest ethical standards becomes even stronger. If business leadership imposes that type of obligation, quite obviously a nation that finds itself the leader of the free world faces obligations far more profound and pervasive.

The basic responsibility of this nation is to protect its own strength. Upon this rests our ability to perform all our other responsibilities. In this showdown struggle between freedom and despotism the United States is the dynamo—the generator of power. If the dynamo stops, or even if it slows up, the lights will go out all over the world. The dynamo can, of course, be overloaded; if it is, it will break down. That is why we must avoid taking on commitments that cannot be met. And the force of the dynamo can be impaired by the short circuits of wrangling among ourselves.

In the emergency period in which we find ourselves we must remain united. We cannot afford to indulge in the luxury of blaming a particular party or group of individuals for our present troubles. We should be too busy to search for scapegoats. If we do, we may lose our future by looking at the past. We should all admit our common error and concede that the weakness of our present situation is the result of our miscalculations as to Russia's postwar attitude. Most of us thought that after World War II she would join us in seeking peace. I certainly did, and have no apologies for so thinking. We also made the tragic mistake immediately after V-J Day of breaking up the finest army ever put together. We are now inclined to reproach Congress for that action. Speaking personally, I cannot do so in clear conscience. Our five sons were all in the service, and I must admit that after V-J Day my wife and I were insistent that our boys be brought home without delay. So were many other mothers and fathers. Perhaps all of us have enough guilt to stop us from pointing a finger at others.

We cannot even begin to fulfill our global obligations without a foreign policy that is bipartisan in fact as well as in name. If that foreign policy is to be effective, the Republican and Democratic parties must co-operate in a spirit of genuine unity of purpose. When we address ourselves to the world we must speak as the voice of the nation and not as that of a single party. I do not for a moment imply that foreign policy should not be forthrightly discussed and debated. But I believe that the vote of every senator and representative should register his individual conviction as an American rather than as a Republican or Democrat. Today there can be no such thing as a Republican foreign policy or a Democratic foreign policy. There can be only an American foreign policy. This is our first responsibility.

The principle of a united backing for our foreign policy is constantly subject to the vagaries of party politics, particularly when the faction in power controls the executive and legislative branches of the government. This also holds true even when control over the White House and the Congress is divided. Most of us remember how, after World War I, partisan opposition to President Wilson's foreign policy, led by Senator Henry Cabot Lodge, fatally weakened the League of Nations even before it got under way by keeping the United States out. But I am proud to say that partisan support of our foreign policy after World War II tremendously increased the power and prestige of our government abroad. The Economic Cooperation Administration was brought into being by the Republican Eightieth Congress with overwhelming support of both parties. And I think it should be set down here, to the credit of a great name, that the present senator from Massachusetts, Henry Cabot Lodge, has striven as vigorously in the past few years for a united foreign policy as his grandfather had against it. Senator Tom Connally also merits unstinted praise for his support of the bipartisan foreign policy—both as the minority leader of the Foreign Relations Committee of the Eightieth Congress and as chairman of that committee in the Seventy-ninth and Eighty-first Congress. So do Republican Charles (Doc) Eaton, a veritable dynamo, and Democrat "Judge" Kee of the House Foreign Affairs Committee.

But the lion's share of the credit for bipartisanship, or unpartisanship, as he likes to call it, belongs to Senator Arthur H. Vandenberg. During his chairmanship of the Senate Foreign Relations Committee, every major vote taken on foreign policy was unanimous—13 to 0.

In March 1950, when the unity of our foreign policy lay in jeopardy, Senator Vandenberg led the rescue party. The spirit of bipartisanship had been deteriorating steadily since the November 1948 elections. This was due, in part, to the failure of the Democratic leaders in the Administration to consult with the Republican leaders in the Senate and House, and in part to the attack on our foreign policy by the isolationists of both parties. I was very much worried. There seemed to be no hope for adequate appropriations for the ECA in that year of acute emergency without support from both parties. I called on Senator Vandenberg to urge him to exert his powerful influence to maintain and to strengthen bi-partisanship. From his sickbed the next day he wrote me an eloquent and forceful letter, which said in part:

ECA was launched as an unpartisan enterprise—established by a *Republican* Congress in full and free co-opera-tion with a *Democratic* Executive. This working *unity* typified our finest traditions and our greatest safety in the presence of external hazards to *all* Americans, regardless of party. You have clung tenaciously to this unpartisan concept in your administration of ECA. As one citizen to another, I thank you for this service from a grateful heart. *United*, we stand. *Divided*, we fall. I want America to *stand*.

Vandenberg's statement deeply impressed almost everyone in Washington and was widely quoted in the press. President Truman quietly began to consult Re-publican leaders again. Secretary Acheson appointed John Foster Dulles, former Republican senator from New York and a key policy-maker, and John Sherman Cooper, former Republican senator from Kentucky, as top-level advisers. The Secretary also arranged for a series of conferences with senators and representatives from both parties. As a result of the galvanic response to Senator Vandenberg's letter, ECA and other foreign policy enterprises again had unqualified, two-party support.

In addition to a constructive bipartisan foreign policy, we owe it to ourselves and to others to safeguard our own domestic economy against further inflation. This is our second responsibility.

A serious inflation in the United States would quickly make itself felt throughout the world. It would nullify one of ECA's major accomplishments—the victory against inflation in Europe. In 1948 fiscal chaos prevailed in most European countries. Today they enjoy financial stability. That stability would be shattered by an increase in prices in the United States, so sharp as to threaten both Europe's recovery gains and its re-armament program. For years we have recognized the pernicious effects of a rapid rise in prices and wages on individuals with fixed incomes—teachers, civil servants, pensioners and those living on annuities. In the present situation, not only these groups but every one of us would be decisively damaged by serious inflation because it would not only add greatly to the cost of defense but would also disrupt and slow down the functioning of our economy at a time when we desperately need maximum efficiency.

We must stop inflation—but how? The root cause of

inflation is, of course, an excess of demand over supply; its cure is to be found in increasing supply, decreasing demand or by a combination of both.

Increased supply is the soundest of all answers to inflationary prices that are due to a real shortage of finished goods and raw materials. In the latter case we should enlarge domestic production and encourage foreign production, particularly in such strategic items as copper, cobalt, chrome, rubber and manganese. The ECA has long been promoting this type of output for stockpiling purposes.

Along the home front the government should offer special incentives to all industry to expand plant capacity. There is one incentive which would cost nothing but which would rapidly foster new construction for producing more goods. I am aware that defense demands must have top priority over steel and other products required for new construction. Yet by a judicious division of materials between the immediate and long-range needs for both the military and civilian sectors of the economy, we can considerably step up our capacity in mine and mill and factory and thus increase our supply sources for every type of commodity. Whatever we can do in this direction, however, is not by itself enough to avoid further inflation.

To cope with this condition it is natural to think first of direct controls, particularly price controls. Unfortunately, price controls alone can neither avert nor check inflation. Indeed, since they keep prices from rising, they make it possible for consumers to buy *more* goods rather than less. For precisely this reason price controls are very apt to lead to rationing. Taken together, price control and rationing limit both what the consumer can buy and what he pays, and bottle up the demand for the rationed item. This in turn increases the demand for unrationed goods. In this way, price controls and rationing spread to more and more commodities. And, to be effective, price controls and rationing must be accompanied by wage controls to help dam back the overflow of purchasing power.

There are many disadvantages to the triumvirate of price control, rationing and wage control. A free economy, by its very freedom, induces a natural balance among a myriad of prices, wages and costs. That balanced relationship is certain to be lost as officials substitute their judgments for the higgling of the market. The end of OPA found our economic system marred by distortions and maladjustments. To my mind, the chief drawback of controls while they are in use is the way they unavoidably impede production. It takes endless time to unravel the red tape of an over-all authority. Even more important is the debilitating effect of over-centralized decision-making. The diffusion of authority which characterizes our free economy is the underlying source of its strength. I have observed that in countries where the right to make decisions is taken away from businessmen they become resigned, apathetic and lacking in the drive so necessary to keep an economy alive and expanding.

Despite these basic objections to direct controls, there are conditions under which they must be imposed, as during the present crisis.

But indirect and impersonal controls should be employed to the greatest extent possible to minimize the use of direct and personal controls. In this respect credit control is of the first importance. Already the Federal Reserve Board requires larger down payments and less time on installment purchases. Mortgage terms for new residential construction have been stiffened, and some building has been forbidden entirely. More can be done in both these fields, and credit may be generally tightened by increasing reserve requirements for the commercial banks and by other measures. The advantage of such credit controls is that when they discourage or prevent a consumer or businessman from spending money he is not left with dammed-up purchasing power that can spill over in other places. These controls also require little policing. Furthermore, they are relatively painless. Their effect is felt throughout the economy, without direct intervention in our personal and business lives.

Controls are not the only methods of cutting down the demand for goods by businessmen and consumers. Government spending can also be reduced, especially the huge outlays of state and local governments for new buildings and the like. The whole country also can and should do more saving. Since the war, the Treasury has conducted a successful campaign for selling United States Savings Bonds. Private financial institutions have also promoted private savings. These activities should be stepped up sharply. However, taxes, in addition to indirect controls, offer our best hope for avoiding inflation in a still relatively unregimented economy. If each American is willing to accept higher taxes which will put our defense program on a pay-as-you-go basis, a vital step will have been made toward fiscal stability and toward keeping the American dollar a symbol of soundness and integrity the world over.

The third responsibility of leadership is to create a program, not national, but international, in scope for the allocation of scarce materials. Only thus can we prevent runaway prices for crucial supplies. It is always difficult to work out international arrangements. But in the case of tin, copper, wool and rubber, an agreement—formal or informal—is necessary to prevent competitive bidding among the nations.

Fourth, as the leader of the free world, the United States must revise its attitude toward foreign trade. The great "giver of peace," Great Britain, in the nineteenth century advanced international stability and amity by means of a world trade that benefited everybody. The United States must build to the same end. For a century we have hidden behind our tariff walls, protecting our "infant industries," bulwarked by the self-sufficiency of our immense resources. We have sold to the world but have been reluctant to buy from it, and world trade has been thrown badly out of balance. Moreover, the recent failure of our imports to expand proportionately to our national output has intensified that imbalance. The real volume of goods imported into this country between 1929 and 1948–49 increased only 5 per cent at the same time that the real domestic output (our national farm and factory production) increased 60 per cent. Under such circumstances other nations could not afford to continue buying from us unless we gave them money. And that is, of course, exactly what we have had to do through a dozen loan and grant schemes, starting from after World War I right down to our present ECA. American aid to Western Europe during the last thirty-five years has amounted to some $22,000,000,000 exclusive of direct war outlays. This was—apart from genuine philanthropic motives—a way of subsidizing our exports, for practically all the American money that went abroad never stayed there; it always returned to buy American goods.

To my mind, the only sound basis for world trade is a business basis. If we are to sell goods abroad and get paid for them in dollars, we must give foreign nations an opportunity to earn the dollars they need. Quite obviously, as the world's largest creditor nation, we should welcome increased imports. That means that we should take a hard look at both our tariffs and our customs regulations. Since 1934 we have made some progress in that direction; the reciprocal trade agreements program has done much to lower duties and has repaired much of the damage inflicted by the notorious Smoot-Hawley high-tariff act. But we can go further. We still charge duties of up to 110 per cent on many items. Moreover, the entire procedure for determining them is antiquated and obstructive. Our tariff act has several thousand classifications, many of them capricious and arbitrary. Some imported cotton carpets, for instance, are subject to a 10 per cent duty, but if they have fringe at the ends they may be subject to as much as 40 per cent duty. Often an importer does not know what duty he is paying until after he has *sold* the goods in the United States, for customs authorities reserve the right to change the classification months after the goods have entered this country.

Clearly, Congress should immediately pass the Customs Simplification Act that it now has before it. It should also, I believe, give the President wide discretionary powers to modify customs procedures to cope with special situations. At the present time, in view of our already existing inflation, the President should be allowed to reduce or eliminate duties on scarce items and thus bring prices down. This could be done without serious injury to any American industry or economic group.

We should at once eliminate the "Buy American" gags in our federal statute books that require government agencies to buy domestic as against foreign goods. In my opinion, this provision, which forces higher prices on many defense items, is adding hundreds of millions to the cost of our rearmament program. Moreover, it puts us in the embarrassing and inconsistent position of discriminating against foreign goods at the same time that we urge non-discrimination upon the rest of the world.

As crimping as "Buy American" legislation is the legal requirement that at least 50 per cent of all US-financed goods destined for foreign countries be transported in vessels of American registry. This has increased the cost of the ECA program by millions of dollars. If the goods had been shipped in the vessels of any of the countries receiving aid, their dollar allotments for commodities could have been increased by the amount of their savings.

It is imperative for the United States to maintain a strong merchant fleet. I am perfectly willing to pay my share of any subsidy to keep such a fleet in being. However, in my view, we should determine the size and composition of the fleet we need only after we have taken into account the capacity of such nations as Norway, Belgium, the Netherlands and Great Britain to furnish shipping for the common defense of the Atlantic Community. Once having made that determination, let us pay any subsidy that may be necessary, but let it be open and not concealed.

Perhaps the Achilles heel of our foreign trade is our domestic agricultural policy. Like Topsy, it has been allowed just to grow, over the past three decades, with little thought to its impact on the rest of the world and even to its long-range impact upon our own economy, agricultural and otherwise. Yet agriculture is basic to all world economies.

The nub of the present policy is the guaranteed minimum price to the farmer for his produce. The guaranteed minimum price was originally designed to protect farmers against loss from a few key crops such as cotton and wheat. But its coverage has been persistently extended until today 51 per cent of farm commodities have been placed under this largest price umbrella in the world.

Currently, most farm commodities are supported at or around 90 per cent of their parity—parity being defined as the price per unit (i.e., a bushel of potatoes or hundredweight of hogs which commands today the purchasing power equal to that of the average price for the same commodity back in either 1910–14 or in the past ten years). The modest level of fifteen years ago has been increased to such an extent that farmers now are guaranteed against much more than severe loss.

This excessive bolstering of farm prices tends to restrict markets both at home and abroad. Consumers cannot afford to buy the entire available supply. Surpluses pile up in warehouses and in caves. And, since American prices are so unrealistically high, overseas farmers are pushed into uneconomic planting of such crops as cotton and wheat, thus reducing US export of these items. This shrinkage in exports, as US farmers price themselves out of the world market, should cause everybody genuine concern. After all, agricultural products have comprised a little over 24.0 per cent of all US exports or thirty-two billion dollars during the past twenty years. Moreover, entire areas in the Southwestern cotton belt, for example, largely depend upon foreign customers. What applies to Texas and Oklahoma in cotton applies to various wheat regions such as Kansas and Washington.

As one who believes that the mainspring of free enterprise is to expand production by means of high volume output at lower unit cost, I cannot help being troubled by the deadening effect on American agriculture which comes from reversing this process. I am convinced that the American farmer, of all people, certainly does not want to become an economic ward of the state. Yet present fixed and rigid prices not only violate the supply-and-demand equation but also foster an ever greater amount of government regulation, intervention and control. The Department of Agriculture, as directed by Congress, has either to impose acreage allotments and marketing quotas to cut production or to siphon off surpluses that cannot be sold at the support price. By mid-1950 the Commodity Credit Corporation, which is the Department of Agriculture's price-support agency, owned or had loans on four and one-half billion dollars' worth of surplus grains, eggs, butter, soybeans and a long list of other farm products. To try to dispose of such surpluses, the department has been compelled to resort to what amounts to "dumping" overseas, a procedure which induces anger on the part of foreign farmers and retaliation by their governments. Closer home, our own farmers are encouraged through price supports to grow more potatoes by the modern techniques, even though the government will buy part of the crop only to destroy it. I recognize that government subsidy of potato destruction represents an extreme example, but it does serve to highlight an essentially unhealthy situation in many other sectors of our farming industry.

It should be emphasized that our agricultural policy

is not unique in its extreme nationalism. The domestic agricultural programs of many other countries also encourage uneconomic output and back up their farmers by measures immediately attractive but eventually dangerous.

In trying to come to grips with the present conflict between domestic farm policy and the aims of our foreign economic policy, I want to make it doubly clear that I believe that in our society the farmer is just as entitled to protection against economic hazards over which he has no control as labor is against unemployment. The point at issue is not whether he should get protection. It is rather how that protection can be worked out in practice to harmonize his interests with an ever-expanding market at home and abroad. I am not a farm economist, but on a common-sense business basis it seems to me that the solution is to be found in the area of more sensitive and flexible price supports. We must allow farm production to gear itself to shifts in demand, and the more automatic this process can be, the better are prospects for economically sound adjustments.

I think that this approach must also be projected into the international sphere. Farm spokesmen for the countries of the free world should be able to sit around the conference table and reach agreement on how continuously to modify internal agricultural programs, bringing them in harmony with today's need for expanding world trade.

I believe that this procedure will get superior results more quickly than, say, world commodity pacts such as the International Wheat Agreement. We must go beyond the mechanics of foreign trade with which such arrangements mainly deal, to a denationalizing of agricultural programs inside the countries of the free world.

It has become increasingly evident that these programs of overprotection in prices, along with tariffs and import quotas, do much to generate foreign hardships and tensions which erupt into autarchy, dictatorship and aggression. The resulting wars and their aftermath cost us thousands of times more, in terms of every type of resource, than the short-run financial gain for our farming population.

Fortunately, there are no more enlightened group leaders in America than the officials of our great farm organizations, the American Farm Bureau Federation, the National Grange, the Farmers Union and the National Council of Farmer Cooperatives. Many times during the past two and a half years I have had the advantage of the advice and counsel of these and other agricultural leaders on Marshall Plan aid to Europe and on programs to rebuild and modernize its agriculture. I have been gratified by the way they recommended and endorsed measures to increase trade in farm and other products as well as to maintain and strengthen the economies of all free nations. They have supported policies that at first glance seemed to run counter to the immediate interests of American farmers, but which upon mature reflection worked decisively to their long-term benefit.

That is why I am particularly confident that farm groups in this country will act on the need to reassess and reshape our agricultural pricing policy. I am sure that they will develop new principles which will continue to safeguard the farmer's basic security while helping to liberate the forces of freer trade throughout the free world.

Even a partial listing of the tremendous responsibilities we have fallen heir to shows how heavy is the burden we must carry as the leading nation of the free world.

During the time when I was ECA administrator I often found myself wishing that there was some practical way we could return to the deceptively "easier" isolationism which marked the period between World Wars I and II. But we can never return. There is no road back. Either we must rise to meet these new responsibilities or the free world will go down. We will have defaulted on our opportunity to wage and win the peace.

CHAPTER 5

Waging the Peace on the Military Front

Perhaps the safest, easiest way for an American to get a glimpse of Russia's martial might is to visit a certain Russian War Memorial which, by an ironic twist, is located in the British sector of Berlin.

It stands west of the Brandenburg Gate, near the gutted ruins of the Reichstag, and grim Russian guards maintain an unbroken vigil before its white pylons.

The entrance is flanked by a huge tank and a long-barreled artillery rifle. These are appropriate, I presume, to a war memorial, yet I find in them another meaning.

When I last looked at these symbols of war, battles were raging in Korea and I knew with a deep and crushing certainty that we of the West could never achieve an enduring peace until the war potential of tens of thousands of Russian tanks and guns like those in front of me had been neutralized by an even greater potential—for peace—on our own side.

I think of myself as a man of peace. I wish with all my heart that we could make peace secure solely by economic, political and other non-violent means. But we all know now that it is useless to bolt the front door if we leave the back door open. The free world can be kept free only by defending itself against any form of aggression.

Here again the responsibility for leadership rests upon the United States. Not only must our Defense Department make our own defenses so invincible that the Kremlin will not dare attack us, but we must also assist the free world to develop its military strength up to a point where the Kremlin would find it suicidal to send its Red armies into Western Europe or Asia. I am not a military expert, but I have associated enough with experts to appreciate the complexity of their task. I also know from personal knowledge how difficult it is to provide necessary finances for our defense effort without endangering our own economy.

The primary function of our Army, Navy and Air Force is to defend the United States and its possessions. In view of world trends today, this assignment cannot be confined to the territorial area of the United States. It is not true that we can best defend ourselves by limiting military action to the protection of our own soil. To throw radar rings about Rapid City and anti-aircraft batteries around Keokuk might prove to be the most *inefficient and costliest of defenses.* In these days of long-range aircraft and atom bombs, in this dawning era of guided missiles, the best defense of the American Midwest might well be in Berlin, Tokyo or Spitsbergen.

Any attack against an ally is an attack on us. That is why ours is a dual challenge—to arm ourselves and our allies to the utmost, for the free world has only a single frontier.

Our own security rests upon the security of others. This was recognized as a central part of national policy when President James Monroe, in his famous doctrine, gave warning to the Old World that the United States would not tolerate further intervention in the Americas. At that time, because no machinery existed for carrying on conversations with our Latin-American neighbors, Monroe issued his warning as a *unilateral* gesture. Today we have the mechanism of the Pan American Union for bringing about agreements in this hemisphere, and the principle of collective security was adopted in the Inter-American Treaty of Reciprocal Assistance at the Rio conference in 1947, when all American republics agreed to join in the defense of any member.

Under the Mutual Defense Assistance Program we have entered into defense arrangements with the Philippines, Korea and "the general area of China" in the

69

Far East, Iran, Greece and Turkey in the Middle East. Under the North Atlantic Treaty Organization we, and Canada, have joined forces with most of Western Europe—the United Kingdom, Norway, Denmark, Belgium, the Netherlands, Luxembourg, France, Portugal, Italy and Iceland—in common defense against any aggressor. Moreover, as a member of the United Nations we have, when called upon, the solemn obligation to "take such action by air, sea or land force as may be necessary to maintain or restore international peace and security."

Moreover, the UN now can call an emergency session of the General Assembly after the outbreak of hostilities anywhere, if the Security Council—because of some country's exercise of the veto—is unable to take action against any such threat to the peace. The emergency session can be convoked within twenty-four hours upon the request of any seven members of the Security Council or by majority vote in the UN (this new procedure makes it easier to break the bottleneck of Soviet vetoes). Furthermore, under an American proposal now pending, the UN eventually may be in a position to count on crack UN units recruited from the armed forces of its member states. It is hoped that this world-wide security force can swiftly act in concert to thwart aggression at the very moment it gets under way.

We *do not* have enough troops now, nor will we have

in the foreseeable future, to safeguard all the world's "soft spots," many of which, such as Indo-China, Burma, Afghanistan, Iran and others, lie along the fringes of the Soviet orbit. Nor have we taken the view that it is in the interest of the United States to risk all-out war in defense of every threatened nation. We do not intend to dilute our strength by spreading ourselves in a thin straggling line around the world.

Our own armed strength, together with that of NATO and UN units and other potential allies, could convince the Kremlin that the risks of general war are too great for Soviet survival.

At the heart of the free world's defense is NATO. In my opinion it is the right and natural answer to a Europe in which nationalism has reached a historic height and is now on the decline. The citizens of many European countries would rather fight under the banner of a United West than under their own flags. They realize that if each were to stand by itself alone it would be readily vanquished, that its best guarantee of security is all for one and one for all, banding together for common purposes under a common command. NATO is also the best approach to the problem of using the man power and productive might of Western Germany.

During its first year NATO has been besieged with problems of organization. It has been even encumbered with boards and committees whose functions have often overlapped and have often needed to be clarified. One of its more obvious deficiencies has been the lack of a unified top authority and a supreme commander. Fortunately for us all such an authority has been created, and even more fortunately, the logical man to head it up—General Eisenhower—has agreed to get back into uniform and do the job. He has the ability to inspire, the diplomacy to gain assent and the toughness to get things done which can do much to develop a European Army into both shield and buckler for the West. Let's pause right here and calculate our own strength as against that of the Soviet Union.

In terms of population, of course, we are least impressive. But in many important items we outstrip both the Kremlin and its satellites. The United States will have in 1951 the physical capacity to produce 95,000,000 metric tons of crude steel per year and Western Europe 55,000,000. The Soviet sphere will probably be able to produce only 33,000,000 metric tons. The United States can produce if necessary between 600,000,000 and 700,000,000 metric tons of coal as against Western Europe's 450–500,000,000 and an annual output in the Soviet and its satellites of less than 400,000,000. The United States will have the capacity to produce 45,000,000 metric tons of cement in 1951 as against Western Europe's 50,000,000 tons and the Soviet sphere's 13,000,000.

The United States can produce about 2,300,000,000 barrels of oil and Western Europe about 25,000,000. In addition, the remainder of the free world, in South America, the Near East and the Far East, can produce an additional 2,000,000,000 barrels. The Soviet Union and its satellites will probably produce in 1951 about 350,000,000 barrels. The United States will probably turn out 400,000,000,000 KWH of electricity in 1951 and Western Europe 250,000,000,000 as contrasted with some 140,000,000,000 KWH by the USSR and its satellites. Other standard indices of the West's productive strength, from locomotives to tractors, are far ahead of Soviet production levels. And let no one who reads these figures fail to note what a vital proportion of our production potential is provided by Western Europe. Let those "realists" who would abandon Western Europe to its fate remember that if Western Europe were taken over intact by the Kremlin, and its resources added to those of the Soviet sphere, the net result would be that the resources controlled by the Kremlin would in many essentials equal those of the United States. I think this is proof positive that we cannot wage the peace by ourselves.

Our industrial power is already matched by military power to an extent not perceived by our hysteria-mongers. Here in the United States we are ahead of the procession, for example, in our experiments to develop such advanced tactical weapons as atomic war heads and artillery. We are in fact stronger than we think. To be sure, in terms of man power already mobilized, the Soviet sphere is ominously superior for the moment. It can today put into the field of combat some 6,400,000 men, fully trained, equipped and dependable, as against the partially trained, equipped and dependable non-Communist alignment of some 3,175,000. But in sea power, whose decisive importance has been again underscored by the Korean campaign, the non-Communist world has the overwhelming advantage of six million tons of fleets in being as against the one-half million tons of the Communists. In air power the non-Communist world has 38,000 planes, or 9,000 more than the Soviet Union can draw on.

In Western Europe proper, of course, the military weakness of the free world has been most dramatically in evidence. Great Britain, France, Italy, the Lowlands and other nations of the West are now only beginning to rearm. The Soviet Union could today hurl 1,000,000 men against 100,000, and 45,000 tanks against 5,000. Moreover, in France and Italy, Communist influence would insure widespread sabotage and disruption of transport, communications and industry in general if war with Russia should occur.

Why then haven't the Russians marched toward the Atlantic? Or do they plan to march soon now because we are obviously at the lowest point of our war potential for many years to come? I have sought answers to these questions all over Europe, of Churchill and Bevin, of Dirk Stikker of the Netherlands, of Giuseppe Pella of Italy and of Paul van Zeeland of Belgium. They do not expect the Red Army to roll within the near future. The reasons they give are varied.

Foremost in almost everyone's mind (and Churchill placed his main reliance on this) was the belief that our bigger and better stockpile of atom bombs and our swift moves toward the creation of the H-bomb were telling deterrents to any Red Army adventure. Everyone I met was heartened by the United Nations' prompt response to aggression in Korea. The Kremlin knows unmistakably that it cannot march into Western Europe without precipitating full-scale war.

These are factors of power and mechanics. The Europeans, who know the Russians far better than we do, also pointed out certain political and ideological brakes to a major Russian aggression. The Kremlin, they say, has a cynical respect for world opinion. The Kremlin is aware that any aggressive move in Western Europe would finally and irrevocably turn all of the free world against the Soviet Union. To exhibit such naked and open aggression would particularly damage the Soviet case in Asia, where the Communists pose as nationalists and liberators. The tolerance displayed by many Indians,

75

Pakistani and Burmese toward Communist tactics would be sharply reversed by any such final proof of Soviet imperialist rapacity.

Moreover, Europeans argue, the Soviet leadership considers a major war to be unnecessary at the present time. The Politburo still believes in the Marxist doctrine that the capitalist world has within it basic conflicts and contradictions which will eventually bring about its collapse. Even though the predictions of a number of Soviet soothsayers, probably now in jail, that we would be up against economic catastrophe in 1946, 1948 and 1949 have failed to materialize, the hope persists in Moscow that Communism can wait it out and ultimately pick up the pieces of broken capitalism. For the Politburo is sure that time is on its side. But the Politburo is unsure that it has all the trained man power it needs to hold down the resistance movements which would undoubtedly surge up if Soviet armies were to overrun and try to dominate all Europe. At the same time, the Kremlin is not particularly anxious again to expose Soviet troops to the comparative luxuries of Western life.

In the last few months of World War II the Soviet soldier got a quick appreciative look at the superior living standards of even the war-impoverished countries to the west of Russia's boundary line. He was flabbergasted by the incredible luxury which surrounded his

American counterpart, the latter's watches, food, shoes, uniforms, his chocolate, cigarettes and pay check.

Finally, Stalin knows very well that the downfall of Hitler and Mussolini resulted directly from the full-scale war touched off by invasion of free countries. To take a chance in the light of such precedents, of such long-shot odds, is not in line with Stalin's previous strategy. He knows that the other two totalitarian dictatorships and their leaders perished because of an unsuccessful war of their own making. In fact, when Averell Harriman was our postwar Ambassador to Russia, Stalin said to him during a Kremlin conference, "Hitler's great mistake was to get involved in a long war."

Of course these speculations do not guarantee that the Russians will not start World War III. Nor are they reasons for complacency. But they do offer the hope for a few decisive years in which to build up our defensive military strength to the point where the Red Army will not dare march. By 1953 we must, in the opinion of the best military minds, build up an American force of three to four million men under arms. This force must be in a state of instant readiness reinforced by enormous reserves backed by a 1,000-ship fleet and a 100-group air force. We must help the Europeans build up a defense force of at least fifty divisions, designed, in case of war, to check the Soviets east of the Rhine for at least three months until massive American aid can arrive. Furthermore, we will be obliged to aid the United Nations to bring its security forces up to some five divisions, aided by fast transport to rush them to endangered areas.

This will take money. For the next three years, at the least, we will have to spend in the neighborhood of fifty billion dollars annually. This figure includes four to six billion dollars allocated to Europe through the Mutual Defense Assistance Program, and a billion or more for Asia. Such sums are necessary if we are to assume what George Washington long ago called a "posture of defense." What this means is a defense which either dissuades the enemy from attack or enables us to prevent a knockout blow. Of this fifty billion dollars, some fifteen billion will go for the new equipment required by our own enlarged armed forces. Fortunately, much of this new equipment will represent what business calls "capital outlay," material which requires only infrequent replacement. Thus, after the third year, and when our armed forces have been beefed out to a "posture of defense," we will be able to prune our spending to some twenty to twenty-five billion dollars a year until the world reaches a durable peace.

The relationship between what we spend on defense and our gross national product ($279,000,000,000 in 1950) is a very sensitive one. As I have already pointed out, too large an outlay for military forces over a long period would endanger our economy (by encouraging either excessive inflation or forcing a full paraphernalia of controls). Hence, our military spending should be kept within limits which will permit America to continue to increase its productive power—a power that is based on a free and expanding economy.

I think that if we can hold our defense spending to the levels I have suggested, and can sharply reduce them after the third year, we will not seriously endanger our economy. But to do this we must change some of our ideas of soldiering. Right now the average American private is paid about three dollars a day, plus allowances for medical, dental care, et cetera. Make no mistake about it, he needs it. For many of our boys in uniform have been taken away from their families and are the sole means of support of young wives and children. But if we are to prepare a defense that will hold off Red aggression, we need three million soldiers, sailors, marines and airmen in uniform and ready to shoot. Yet we simply can't pay them three dollars a day (and colonels up to eight thousand dollars a year) and stay within that twenty to twenty-five-billion-dollar-a-year bracket that the country is able to carry over the long term. The answer is Universal Military Training. Here is how it would work. At the age of about eighteen *all* male Americans, before they have assumed family obligations, will go into armed-force training establishments for a two-year hitch. They will be given good care, food and clothing, and enough pay for incidental expenses, perhaps a dollar a day. (A Turkish soldier gets one dollar a month in cash and a French bachelor colonel gets two hundred dollars a month.) When they are released, at twenty, they can return to their jobs or continue their schooling. At the same time they become a well-trained reserve whose existence will eventually enable us to reduce the size of our standing army.

This training for war in time of peace is not a process that comes easily to anti-militarist Americans. Yet only by recognizing the scope of the disaster that awaits us if we falter, and by agreeing to sacrifice convenience and comfort in order to retain freedom, can we or our ideal of freedom manage to survive.

We will not be the only ones to devote a large share of national income to defense.

United waging of the peace will call for immense spending on the part of the Western Europeans. During 1951–52 they will have to spend from twelve to thirteen billion dollars of their own money for adequate military defense.

Fortunately, as a result of her remarkable recovery, Europe's plants are again in good shape. The wheels are turning, and the war materials will come rolling off the production lines. Without Marshall Plan aid, our allies in Western Europe would be in no position to rearm themselves effectively. For this reason, as well as for reasons of economic stability and morale, we must continue whatever assistance may be needed to enable them to complete specific programs for economic recovery, especially those already under way. Otherwise, we will see steel plants and power projects half finished, with a corresponding loss in the ability of Western Europeans to forge their own weapons. On this point I am always amazed by those who fail to grasp the connection between economic strength and military strength. Some otherwise intelligent people seem to think that bazookas and tanks, planes and cruisers spring into existence like Minerva from the head of Jove. They do not perceive that the production line is always behind the firing line. Yet Stalin knows this well. "Production wins wars" is among his favorite maxims.

To be sure, the Marshall Plan was not designed to contribute to Western Europe's capacity to produce war matériel. The Marshall Plan in its origin was a plan to achieve a stable prospering economy in all Europe as a major step toward a stable prospering world economy. But from the first, Soviet refusal to participate in the Marshall Plan limited its operations to Western Europe and non-Soviet spheres elsewhere. And more recently, as the Soviet Union's warlike imperialist goals have become unmistakably clear, Western Europe along with the rest of the free world has been forced, out of sheer self-preservation, to undertake large-scale preparations for defense. The extent to which the Marshall Plan has helped to develop a healthy Western European economy as the indispensable basis for the output of military supplies is exemplified by the case history of a new self-propelled field gun that the French are now making. Into it go steel, lead, petroleum, ball bearings; behind it are strip mills, mechanized coal mines, railroads with new rolling stock and many other products and industrial facilities.

Consider steel, for example. In 1945 steel production in France and the Saar had dropped to 1,500,000 tons; but today as a result of the Marshall Plan it is 10,000,000, or 8,500,000 tons more, while French steel capacity is being rapidly expanded for gun barrels, among other things. Similarly, France in 1950 was able to manufacture some 350,000 autos and trucks, twice its prewar figure; and the assembly lines for these can be converted to turn out engines and chassis for the self-propelled field gun. By the same token a new factory in the Haute-Savoie, set up with Marshall Plan aid, can furnish ball bearings and other moving parts; and France has virtually doubled her tire production since the Marshall Plan has made it possible for her to import carbon black and machinery that can mold the huge tires for the gun. Lubricants for it are assured by France's ability to refine twice as much petroleum as before World War II; shells and brass gun sights and cogs will come in part from a new Moroccan mine developed under the Marshall Plan to produce 85,000 tons of lead and 120,000 tons of zinc annually. And so it goes, from the Marshall Plan-sponsored revival in the textile industry which can provide gun covers to more efficient coal mines that provide coke for steel furnaces to turbines that provide power to turn lathes and drills and to operate punch presses.

There can be no question but that the new military potential of France, like that of other Western European nations, has become a most significant, if unintentional, by-product and extra dividend of the Marshall Plan.

But what about the Europeans' will to fight? That concerns most Americans. It concerns me. Has not that will been sapped by two world wars within a generation, by civil commotion since 1919, by Nazism and Fascism and Communism, by bombings and occupations and, above all, by lack of confidence in the future?

Millions of Western Europeans see themselves caught between two colossi, the United States and the Soviet Union. They see their countries as potential battlegrounds. Are they not therefore tempted toward the spineless doctrine of "neutrality" in France and elsewhere?

From Norway to Turkey I have searched for an answer to these disturbing questions. I didn't find it in definitive terms, but of this much I am certain: all

Europeans, and that includes even the Junkers of Germany, have no stomach for launching a new aggression. They have only abhorrence for the idea. Those who remember the utter devastation of Europe in 1945, after six years of war, can understand this.

Resisting aggression is something else. I can say with assurance that a substantial majority of the peoples closest to the Soviet sphere are willing to fight, and to die, for their homelands. They are without illusions. They know that conquest by the Kremlin means degradation and enslavement—they prefer death. I saw for myself the existence of this resolute spirit in Greece, in Turkey, in western Berlin and in Norway. I received reliable reports of it from Finland. The Finns, by all accounts, are the toughest burr in the hide of the Russian bear. "How," I asked a Norwegian cabinet officer, "are the Finns, who live under the shadow of Soviet power, who make no pretension of their dislike for Communism, who had the temerity to dismiss their Communist cabinet ministers, able to maintain their independence?"

"They are," answered the Norwegian, "very much like a weed that Norwegians call 'brennenesle' and that you call 'nettles,' very spiny and uncomfortable to the touch. The Russians could swallow them, all right, but they could never digest them. The Russians know that and they leave them alone."

Probably no other Europeans are as nettlish as the Finns. But in all of Europe there are millions of people who would rather die on their feet than live on their knees. We must justify their faith that the United States will not blunder into preventive war and that the Kremlin, faced with a United West, will not start an aggressive war.

On both scores there is hopeful news. Nothing finer could have occurred to persuade Europeans that we are in earnest about building up our defenses, and using them to avert war, than the appointment of George Marshall as Secretary of Defense. They vividly remember his leadership in World War II. They look upon him, and rightly, as a military genius who can construct and conduct a great common defense. At the same time they have an immense regard for him as the author of the Marshall Plan as a program for peace. In the same way that he conceived of economic strength as a means of thwarting internal Communist aggression he will conceive of military strength as a means of thwarting external Communist aggression.

My considered judgment is this: if we build up our defense, continue to strengthen Europe economically and militarily, and make clear, as has President Truman on every occasion, that our purpose is peace, we can count on the Europeans to stand side by side with us, to fight if necessary and to win.

CHAPTER 6

Waging the Peace on the Economic Front

In one very real sense, today's contest between freedom and despotism is a contest between the American assembly line and the Communist party line. In this arena the ECA is America's boldest experiment in waging the peace. To support its activities the American people, through their Congress, have already appropriated more than $12,000,000,000 for European recovery, $230,-000,000 for Korea and $275,000,000 for the rest of Asia.

ECA is also the story of the most meaningful two and a half years in my own life. The story began on a bright April day in 1948 when we started operations in Room W-900 in Washington's Hotel Statler. Its inspiration and its challenge carried through from the first feverish weeks of combing the country for men of top talent, during harried periods when we were beset by one crisis after another, through great moments of victory and right up to the day in late October 1950 when I returned from my last trip to Europe, walked into my office in the Maiatico Building for the last time and turned in my papers.

I wish I could unfold the whole pageant of ECA. It is a great and thrilling one—for me, for the hundreds whose almost religious energy and devotion to a cause made the word "bureaucrat" something to be proud of and for the millions of Europeans to whom American aid gave hope and opportunity and often life itself. Unfortunately, I must limit ECA's part in this book to those aspects which illustrate the broad principles that must guide us in waging the peace through future foreign aid programs.

Before outlining the lessons of ECA, I think we should revive, for the benefit of those readers whose memory of 1948's clamorous headlines has faded, a picture of the problems we faced.

The year 1948 was a fateful one for Western Europe, menaced by Kremlin conspiracies. No less an authority than British Foreign Secretary Ernest Bevin has said that Western Europe was on the verge of collapse. And some well-informed correspondents were predicting throughout the spring of that year that within a matter of months—possibly weeks—Western Europe would be dominated by Soviet Russia.

There was ample ground for this pessimism. Already the Red wave had moved west from its own frontiers. It had swept over the once-independent states of Czechoslovakia, Poland, Hungary, Bulgaria and Rumania. Fifth columnists were hard at work in France, Italy and Germany. In all these countries the Communists were getting to be perilously strong. They were busy exploiting the hunger and the hopelessness and the lack of jobs among tens of millions of people. Broken factories were operating fitfully and often slowed to a halt for lack of raw materials and repair parts for equipment. Farmers raised little more than enough to feed themselves. The transport system was in too sad a state of disrepair to carry even the slight food surpluses to undernourished city dwellers. Farmers, lacking faith in the inflated currencies, refused to sell their produce. To compound all these troubles, Western Europe found itself host to millions of refugees and displaced persons who had fled the Kremlin's terror in Eastern Europe.

Such was life in Western Europe in 1948.

It is enough to say that less than three years later—Western Europe's industrial production has been lifted, not merely to prewar levels, but to some 40 per cent above them. The output of crude steel has been increased 25 per cent, motor vehicles about 87 per cent and textile yarns one-third. Farmers in 1950 had bumper crops, and livestock products have reached

89

the prewar standard. Total agricultural production in 1950–51 will probably reach a level of 9 per cent above pre-Marshall Plan days. And production of electric power has gone up 95 per cent. Trains are running again in Europe. Currencies are stabilized. People are eating regularly and working hard; let no one tell you that they are not. This comeback has been called "the most courageous in history," and I support that verdict.

It is from the record of this comeback that I wish to draw the four great lessons that must become the signposts of the future.

WE CAN HELP ONLY THOSE WHO HELP THEMSELVES. Even during those rushed, early days of planning and in the difficult months of putting the program across, we at ECA never had the slightest disagreement on one vital matter—the basic concept of the job itself. General Marshall had said at Harvard: "It would be neither fitting nor efficacious for this government to undertake to draw up unilaterally a program designed to place Europe on its feet economically. This is the business of the Europeans. . . . The role of this country should consist of friendly aid in the drafting of a European program and of later support of such a program so far as it may be practical for us to do so." These vital words, then, became our text: Only the Europeans themselves can save Europe. ECA has never departed from the idea that those who receive aid should accept responsibility for making it count, for making the most of it.

In putting that idea into action, we were immensely aided by the remarkable "counterpart" clause that Congress had written into ECA legislation. Whether Congress knew just what a happy recovery tool it had devised in counterpart, or had simply tossed it in, hoping it would help us watch our dollars, I cannot say. But I can say flatly that it made the difference between success and failure for the Marshall Plan in every nation that had a shaky government, and it helped mightily with those that had strong ones. It was, I believe, the indispensable idea—the essential catalyst.

In briefest outline, the counterpart arrangement requires all governments receiving outright grants to match every dollar with its equivalent in their own currency—in francs, pounds, lire—or whatever. Of this foreign currency, 5 per cent is turned over to the United States Government. It is used for such purposes as running ECA missions to individual countries and purchasing and developing strategic materials for the American stockpile. The remaining 95 per cent is then put into a fund available to the Marshall Plan governments for recovery projects approved by ECA. Thus America's dollars do double duty. They provide the Marshall Plan nations with foreign exchange for vital commodities and they encourage the governments of those nations to use the counterpart—which is currency actually acquired by the sale of those commodities, whether lathes or trucks, to individual buyers—for building up their economies.

If this sounds like fiscal fantasy, let's look at the process in action. The French had made a valiant comeback in their cotton industry, restoring some 80 per cent of prewar capacity. Raw materials ran out. Prior to the Marshall Plan, French millowners faced the threat of having to shut up shop for lack of raw cotton. Unfortunately, France is not a cotton-growing nation and no cotton was available there. The millowners had plenty of francs, but the American cotton grower couldn't use them. Then the Marshall Plan came along. The millowners took their francs to the French exchange control, traded them for dollars (after their requests were approved by French officials and ECA), bought the needed cotton with the dollars and kept their mills going. What about the millowners' francs? They went into the recovery fund and became counterpart—to be used for some such worth-while project as building a highway or creating new farmland by draining a swamp.

What has happened? The dollars kept the French mills active and thousands of French workers at their jobs. They have provided the French Government with a sackful of francs for recovery projects. They have robbed the French Communists of an excellent opportunity to exploit the discontent of idle workers. More importantly, because the French millowners paid for their cotton—and thus ordered only what they needed—the program avoided the waste that is normal in most "giveaway" plans.

WE MUST USE GUIDED DOLLARS. As most Americans know, we have been extending to Europe a vast amount of aid ever since World War I.

In 1947, Congress was facing the task of further aid to Europe. But it wanted to put it on a sounder, more solid basis than ever before. Hence Congress made this the central aim of Marshall Plan legislation. In my opinion, its efforts were notably successful, with good reason: the problem in Europe had been thoroughly studied by congressional investigators (such as the traveling committee headed by the brilliant Christian A. Herter of Massachusetts). The ECA legislation itself was based upon some of the most protracted hearings in congressional history—the testimony filled five volumes and contained 6,584 pages. When the law finally emerged from these hundreds of necessary but wearisome hearings and conferences, it included among its provisions a directive that the European nations: (1) submit a detailed program of their needs, (2) discuss with the ECA administration the trade and fiscal policies they would follow and (3) allow ECA to make end-use checks to determine that American aid was spent as agreed.

The new principle set forth in this legislation is what I call that of "guided dollars." To anyone who might complain that such provisions were arbitrary or uncharitable, I should like to point out that they are actually nothing more than the realistic lending policies of your local banker (I don't claim he's always charitable) transferred to the international stage; or, better yet, it may be compared to the role of a good friend who is willing to finance his neighbor's business venture but who asks first for a thorough explanation of the project to see whether it makes sense, and second for the opportunity to see how it is going from time to time.

A short case history of Italian recovery offers a prime example of the "guided-dollar" principle.

At war's end, Italy was struggling under more burdens than John Bunyan's famous hero. Fortunately, an interim program of United States aid had been made available, even before the advent of the Marshall Plan. It was, in fact, this program, carried on under the able direction of Ambassador James Dunn during the early months of 1948, that did much to save Italy from going Communist in the elections held in April of that year. And when ECA's Chief of Mission James Zellerbach and his crew arrived that summer they required no long series of conferences to verify the continuing urgency of Italy's need for help. For two decades the nation had exhausted itself in efforts to fulfill Mussolini's mad ambition to be the first of the new Roman emperors. Then Italy had gone into the war as a part of the Axis, had been drubbed in Africa, had faltered at home, was taken over by the Germans and was finally invaded by the Allies. Her towns and factories were severely bombed and shelled. The results were plain on the gaunt faces of the Italians, in their exhaustion, and in their cold homes and bare cupboards.

They needed food and warmth. We shipped wheat and coal. They needed raw materials for the factories that still stood. We shipped cotton and steel and copper.

At the same time, work was begun on the more far-reaching plans to revive and rebuild the nation. After exhaustive study, ECA and the Italian Government agreed upon an over-all recovery program that emphasized (1) machines for gutted factories, (2) power to run the machines and (3) more land and improved land cultivation.

The need for plant replacement was obvious. Without the great presses, looms, forges and other equipment that make up a factory, the country could not produce the goods that people eat, wear and use for transportation.

A good example of the job ECA did in getting this program under way was at the Fiat plant at Turin, which had been 75 per cent destroyed during the war. Thanks to a $23,000,000 loan, Fiat obtained new American equipment and is today doing so well that it is producing more than 100,000 passenger cars a year, in addition to a long list of busses and trucks, and has again become one of the automotive leaders of Europe.

At the same time, ECA funds were at work rebuilding Italy's power output. This was a problem, not only of engineering, but of finance. Italy's coal deposits are poor; to import coal would be to lose foreign exchange. One answer was to harness more of the water that fell through the Alpine gorges of the north. This made good sense, and new generating equipment was ordered. But even the Alps have occasional snowless years, and the Italians wanted a hedge against that kind of failure. Accordingly, the Italian investment and import programs have placed heavy emphasis on projects for thermal-generating plants to insure sufficient stand-by capacity and to safeguard production against threat of electricity shortages.

In a remote section of Tuscany, about forty miles south of Florence, they found their insurance: "geothermic power." There, for years, huge jets of steam, the product of water seeping through semi-porous rock to deep-lying lava beds, had erupted into the air. Even before the war, Italian engineers had drilled through those "underground boilers" and harnessed the pent-up steam pressure to produce electricity. Then the retreating Germans had blasted their work to rubble. By the time ECA arrived on the scene, Italian engineers were constantly rebuilding but in desperate need of new piping and turbines. ECA not only provided these but encouraged the Italians to enlarge greatly their geothermic power plants by drilling new wells. Today the plants can produce around 2 billion kilowatt hours of electricity a year, one-twelfth of Italy's total power production.

The land problem is more complex. ECA has helped raise soil yields. Farm mechanization has been encouraged, modern fertilizers introduced and experts sent to show Italian farmers how to control pests and parasites.

In Italy, however, raising agricultural output is not enough. Land is a social, political and mathematical conundrum. Along with the question of absentee landlords, whose large feudalistic estates could and should be divided and sold to working farmers, is the problem of the tens of thousands of small farmers who are trying to eke out a living on two or three acres or even tinier parcels. These are often uneconomically divided into widely separated plots. Thus Italy must not only break up large tracts but consolidate smaller ones. Challenging as the job is, it must be done if the Italian peasant is to be brought to feel that he has a stake in his society.

At the same time, steps must be taken to see that the land acquired by the peasants—often neglected or unfarmed over many years by its previous owners—is developed to the point that it can be productively tilled. This requires large-scale public works in irrigation, drainage, reclamation and roads, as well as making available to new owners the tools and credit to improve their own plots. To meet this double challenge of land improvement and land reform, ECA is using one of the most potent weapons in its economic arsenal—its influence over counterpart funds.

With more than two hundred projects in the works, the agricultural counterpart program is sizable. It extends from Sardinia (where a co-operative ECA-Rockefeller Foundation venture is ridding the island of its centuries-old scourge of malaria) to the fertile plains of the Po and on down to the rocky toe of Calabria. ECA reclamation and irrigation projects are going forward in the Scilla area of Calabria, where the first land redistribution was made by the Italian Government. It was here that the ceremonies marking Italy's first land division took place in the fall of 1950. Three hundred and ninety-six lucky peasants, whose names had been drawn by lot from a box, took possession of nine-acre plots—the first bit of land most of them had ever owned. With tears in his eyes, their leader voiced their thanks: "Since the world began, we never thought to see so luminous a day."

The land that has thus fallen to a few peasants is only the promise of a beginning, a portent of what should be done on a large scale despite all the difficulties of this overpopulous nation which each year adds 400,000 inhabitants to its census rolls.

A HARDHEADED ADMINISTRATION OF AID IS NECESSARY. To hold down the cost of foreign aid programs to a reasonable level and to insure worth-while results, we need tightfisted administration. Loosely administered programs are wasteful. They hurt rather than help the countries they seek to strengthen. Whatever success we may have had with the Marshall Plan is due in part to the fact that, even though we were spending billions, we watched our pennies. The original estimate of the program's cost was seventeen billion dollars. Total appropriations will not exceed thirteen billion dollars for economic recovery which in certain countries has already been largely achieved. In the case of Great Britain aid was suspended on January 1, 1951, eighteen months ahead of schedule.

WE MUST EXPORT OUR SKILLS AS WELL AS OUR DOLLARS. While it is unquestionably true that the secret of America's tremendous industrial production lies largely in the efficient and powerful machines that back up our workers, it is also true that our ingenuity in putting these machines to the best use has accomplished wonders. The special skills and short cuts that our American workers and technicians have learned the hard way are often referred to as "know-how." The

99

export of this, and the import of foreign "know-how" is the basis of the "technical assistance" (TA) program at ECA.

My own concern with raising European productivity (output per man-hour), which I have always considered the only possible way to achieve genuine prosperity for Europe, goes back to 1928. Albert Russel Erskine, president of the Studebaker Corporation, had asked me to make a report on Studebaker's London sales and repair depot, then operating at a loss. When I reached England I was astounded to find that, although wages in London were about half what they were in South Bend, Indiana, the prices on most repair jobs were about double. For example, the South Bend price for a valve-grinding job was around ten dollars. Out of this, the mechanic—who naturally used a power grinder—got four dollars, or an average of eighty cents an hour. Profit to the shop, after overhead, was about one dollar. In London three workers had a part in the operation: an apprentice who did most of the work, a mechanic who actually did the final seating of the valve and an inspector who checked the job. The total labor cost was over eight dollars. Cost to the customer was eighteen dollars. Loss to Studebaker, after overhead, was two dollars.

My first reaction was to suggest the introduction of power tools in the London depot and the improvement of shop practices—along with a lowering of repair charges and a raising of wages. But Studebaker superintendents in London and others in England convinced me that I would come a cropper. Any attempt by a brash American to change traditional practices, they said, would result in disaster. Consequently, I advised President Erskine to sell the London depot, which he did.

But I never forgot what I had seen in London, and through the years that followed, the conviction kept burning within me that the adoption of American labor and management practices would be a great boon to European labor, European management and the European consumers. My chance to do something about it came one warm summer day in Paris in 1948. Sir Stafford Cripps, Britain's ascetic Chancellor of the Exchequer, and I were talking over the economic recovery obstacles that lay ahead. "If we are to raise the standard of living in Great Britain," he said, "we must have greater productivity." My heart quickened; this was the kind of talk I wanted to hear from a European. Then he continued. "Great Britain has much to learn about that from the United States and"—he paused—"I think we have a few manufacturing secrets we've been concealing for a generation or so that you might like to learn. Why don't we interchange this information?"

Naturally, I jumped at the idea. "Let's set up a system of transatlantic visits," I replied. "We can take British management and labor on tours of American factories and send Americans to Britain for a look at your shops." Sir Stafford made the deal right there, and within weeks he had thrown his amazing vegetarian energy into the creation of an Anglo-American Council of Productivity. Top figures like Philip Reed of General Electric and Victor Reuther of the CIO were enlisted to represent American management and labor. The late Sir Frederick Bain, deputy chairman of the Board of Imperial Chemical Industries, and Lincoln Evans, general secretary of the Iron and Steel Trades Confederation, were brought in for the British. Together they settled upon the industries which would benefit most from an exchange of ideas and soon laid out plans and schedules.

The first British team to arrive in the United States represented labor and management in the steel industry. This group spent six weeks over here, exploring our factories, taking notes by day and chewing over them in the evenings. These were no junketeers; they came with determination to learn. When they returned to England they sat down and wrote a report so much of an eye-opener that it sold twenty-five thousand copies in a fortnight and went into three extra printings. Its gist: productivity per man in American foundries was from 50 to 90 per cent higher than in British foundries; the latter must mechanize and raise output or national living standards could not rise as they should.

With this auspicious start in Britain, I had high hopes

that the technical assistance idea would be embraced with equal enthusiasm by other countries. It did not happen that way. Perhaps language difficulties on the Continent blunted perception of what TA could do to modernize the industrial process. From the standpoint of its infinite potentialities, TA has not accomplished as much as it should. On the other hand, some three thousand Europeans, either in teams or in groups of twos and threes, have been given a grounding in American techniques under ECA's Technical Assistance Program. They have not been confined to factory people. Dutch farmers came to study grain growing on Iowa farms, Norwegians our coal mines, Italians learned how to raise hybrid corn and Turks analyzed American civil aviation and public-roads building.

When these Europeans return home, they do their best to install in their own private and public enterprises the techniques they have learned. That means breaking tradition—a tough job anywhere. However, their crusading zeal is paying off, and there is in Europe today a new spirit of expansion and growth.

Even more important than what Europeans learn about lathes and plows is what they learn about America. They learned that this is the land of full shelves and bulging shops, made possible by high productivity and good wages, and that its prosperity may be emulated elsewhere by those who will work toward it. But they

103

learned something even more important. They found out for themselves that the "American Way" is a way marked by the primacy of the person in a setting of teamwork. "There appeared to be a most friendly and genuine attitude of co-operation between management and labor," reported a British rayon-weaving unit. "The relations between management and labor in the great majority of mills we visited were excellent. There was often a sense of camaraderie based on mutual respect," observed a British cotton-spinning team. "The big surprise to me," said a French unionist, "was the importance American bosses give to human relations problems. The American employer seems to be a psychologist aware that his prosperity is tied directly with that of the workers." And a Belgian coal-mining team pointed out that "both management and labor have taken steps to give greater efficiency in production and more understanding in relationships." For our part, we learned that technical assistance is a two-way street; that Sir Stafford was right indeed when he suggested that Americans could learn certain manufacturing refinements, whether for cutlery or cabinets, from the British. Above all, peoples on both sides of the ocean gained a better and truer feeling for each other. The American came to know the Britisher for something more than his "I-say-old-boy" stage caricature, and the Briton brought the American into focus as a real human being, dispelling the old stereotype of the Yank as a cross between a cinematic gangster and an uncultivated bumpkin. It is this kind of understanding upon which the free peoples can build their fight to wage the peace.

At the same time we were trying to help increase productivity in Europe with our large-scale technical assistance program we were also experimenting with another sort of technical aid in China. The China Aid Act of 1948 provided for the formation of the five-member JCRR (Joint Commission on Rural Reconstruction) and sponsored a novel attack on conditions behind the growing unrest in rural areas—conditions which had made China (and southeastern Asia) especially vulnerable to Communist agitation.

Chinese and American agricultural survey teams had, in 1946, pin-pointed areas in which rural reform was needed. Cruelly high rents took an average of 50 per cent of the farmer's crop and ranged as high as 80 per cent. Tenancy contracts were a mockery. They could be altered or abolished at the whim of the landlords. Middlemen profits cut the farmers' earnings, and excessive tax and interest rates bit deep into the meager remainder. In the fall of 1948, "hard cores" of Moscow-trained Communists had cleverly transformed the problems of rural China into major political issues. It would be difficult to exaggerate either the magnitude or the significance of this agricultural discontent. Nearly 80 per cent of Asia's 1,250,000,000 (China's 460,000,000 included) are farmers, susceptible alike to the growing demand for rural reforms and to the propaganda of Communist agents who quickly assumed the guise of "agrarian reformers" in matters of political importance.

It was immediately apparent that before any over-all economic stability could be developed as an offset to Communist pressures, basic improvements and reconstruction would first have to be achieved in rural China.

The JCRR was designed to move along that front and to gain three major objectives simultaneously. It began a "social-justice" program to improve health, to insure fair rentals and increase production.

Unlike missions, whose members spend their time at their desks, the JCRR went out into the hills and worked with the people. There they have lived and talked with the peasants, trying to discover their "felt needs." And I do not hesitate to say that not since Lawrence's days in Arabia has a more sensitive or successful venture been carried out by any Westerners in the Near or Far East.

Dr. Raymond T. Moyer, American member of JCRR and chief of ECA's Mission to Formosa, constantly pushed the commission efforts to persuade provincial governors to institute land-tenure reforms. As a result, in several provinces, rent ceilings were set at 37½ per cent of the crop value, comprising reductions from 12½ to 30½ per cent.

Almost immediately, the farmer's attitude changed. Now that he was going to get a better "keep-home" share, he was interested in raising production. Along with this new attitude toward his work came a warm approval of his local government and a sense of participation in it.

It was in the very provinces that the JCRR program had got under way—in Szechwan, Kwangsi and Fukien —that the Communist invaders found some of the most stubborn grass-roots resistance to their drive.

What a different story might have been told in China if this alternative to Communist strategy had been started a few years earlier.

The work of the ECA has everywhere proved, whether in Asia or Europe, the validity of its basic assumptions: Deeds which lay the basis for physical well-being provide the hope and the faith which permit free people to make rational judgments. Economic regeneration leads to regeneration of morale.

The correlation between material benefits and election results in Europe backs up the point. There were, of course, other influences—the revival of pro-democratic political forces, the Church's crusade against Communism, the increasing awareness among all groups of the difference between its rosy propaganda and its ruthless barbarism. Even when all these are taken into account, however, there remains a very definite connection between economic recovery and anti-Communist votes, as the balloting before and after the Marshall Plan attests. In Belgium, for instance, industrial production has gone up 12 per cent. At the same time, Communist strength in the parliament dropped from seventeen seats to ten. In Norway, production is up 23 per cent and Communist seats in the parliament have fallen from eleven to zero. In the Netherlands, where industrial output is up 51 per cent, Communist seats in the provincial assemblies have declined from 10 per cent in 1946 to 5 per cent in 1950. In Denmark, output is up 31 per cent and the Communist showing is down from 12 per cent of the popular vote (in the 1945 national elections) to 4 per cent in the 1950 national elections. In Austria, production has risen almost 140 per cent; Communist mayors elected in thirty cities five years ago were all defeated in the 1950 balloting.

In Britain, as in Switzerland, Communism has never been a serious problem and the Communist party as such is outlawed in Greece, Turkey and Portugal.

Italy and France remain as the supreme scenes of showdown between East and West, and though the final verdict there is still in the balance, we are making gains. In Italy, the very announcement of Marshall Plan aid helped to decrease Communist representation in the government to an appreciable extent, and the 27 per cent hike in industrial output since then has been a hard blow at Communist strength within the labor movement. In France, the advent of the Marshall Plan prevented, in all probability, a Communist take-over. Since then the 29 per cent gain in industrial production has held in check the spread of Communist influence; and, if we continue to help strengthen the French economy, I have no doubt of the eventual victory of democracy over totalitarianism.

One lesson I did not have to learn. THAT WAS THAT AN EFFICIENT ADMINISTRATION DEMANDS TOP-FLIGHT MEN FOR THE TOP JOBS. Congress had allowed us—for staffing ECA—twenty-five jobs that paid $15,000 a year and seventy-five that carried a $10,000 salary. By government standards that was generous, but in the kind of adventure we were in we had to have one hundred men who could command salaries many times that in industry or in the professions. In getting this kind of top competence in the key places, I had the help of M. T. (Tex) Moore, my personal attorney. We spent long hours on the long-distance telephone, and often one of us would fly across the country to nail down a likely prospect. We succeeded beyond our expectations. I am not being modest, only honest, when I say that much of ECA's accomplishment lay in recruiting better men than myself.

My first recruiting success was to get Averell Harriman, then Secretary of Commerce, to take over direction of European operations as ECA's special representative. His intimate knowledge of Europe, gained as Ambassador to Great Britain and Russia and in other key posts, made him ideal for this assignment. I got William C. Foster, then Undersecretary of Commerce, and one of the most gifted and efficient administrators in Washington, to backstop Harriman in Europe as his deputy. The brilliant and knowledgeable Maryland industrialist, Howard Bruce, came out of retirement to become my deputy administrator. Bruce came with a promise to stay for six months and generously stayed eighteen. As general counsel for the European operations we enlisted Milton Katz, an outstanding Harvard law professor who had served with distinction through the Washington alphabetical labyrinth during World War II.

We not only concentrated on getting men of extraordinary ability for the top jobs but also gave careful attention to building a staff that was truly representative of America—made up of men from all sectors of public and private life. We enlisted men of such diversified backgrounds as Robert Hanes, a commercial banker; Clinton S. Golden, one of labor's genuine statesmen; A. E. Staley, a Midwest industrialist; Richard M. Bissell, Jr., the brilliant M.I.T. economist; Colonel C. Tyler Wood, a former Wall Street broker; and Dr. Dennis FitzGerald, a nationally known food expert from the Department of Agriculture. When we finally got under way ECA boasted a staff that included the best the country could offer from government, labor, business, agriculture and the universities. They delivered in a way that advanced not only the interests of all the American people but also those of the Europeans as well.

From the standpoint of foreign aid programs I believe the most important lesson we have learned is this: to get maximum efficiency out of the dollars we spend abroad, whether they go for recovery, for development of re-tarded economies or for building up military defenses, *one* government agency must have the primary responsibility for allocating all funds. Only by concentrating control over our economic activities abroad in the hands of a single agency can we:

(1) properly apportion aid among countries (several agencies working separately often tend to give one nation too much help, another too little);

(2) avoid waste of dollars within a country (two or more agencies often duplicate functions);

(3) control the impact of our dollars upon the economy of a recipient country (too great a pressure for rearming on a nation of full employment, like Britain, could un-duly drive down the standard of living; the same dollars applied to rearming in a nation of unemployment, like Germany, would raise the standard of living).

The ECA itself has been a pilot plant that has demonstrated how necessary it is to have a single agency in a position to plan simultaneously for economic recovery, economic development and rearmament. To the extent that ECA could exercise authority over these three functions, it was highly successful; to the extent that this authority was divided, its efficiency both in planning and in operations was curtailed.

Therefore, I should like to recommend most urgently to the American people and to Congress that:

An Overseas Economic Administration be formed to administer all aid and technical assistance programs abroad; that this administration have a large measure of control over the policies of such lending agencies as the Export-Import Bank; that United States representatives to all international economic organizations be responsible to it; and that this administration have equal rank with the other departments of the government such as State, Commerce, Interior and that its administrator have cabinet status.

In effect, I recommend that this proposed Overseas Economic Administration take over the present setup of ECA; that it absorb the Point Four program now administered by the State Department; that it supervise at least the economic side of all sums to be spent on European rearmament under the Mutual Defense Assistance

Program. Moreover, American representation in the World Bank, International Monetary Fund, International Trade Organization (when we join) and in all other international government bodies dealing with the world economy would receive its policy direction from such an Overseas Economic Administration.

CHAPTER 7

Waging the Peace on the Political Front

Until recently politics meant little more to me than the Republican and Democratic parties and elections—city, state and national. Furthermore, I had dinned into my ears from early boyhood the idea that we should follow George Washington's advice and avoid all permanent foreign alliances. No one ever mentioned, of course, that in Washington's time it took five weeks to cross the Atlantic and eighteen months for a journey round the world. Today the oceans are the same, but the timetables read a little differently. I have made a number of overnight "commuting" hops across the Atlantic—lunch in New York, breakfast in London or Paris—and I made one trip around the world in fourteen days, spending less than six of them in actual flying time.

I am sure that George Washington, who always courageously faced facts, would be the first to admit that a policy suitable to the world of 1790 could not be applied in 1951. I believe he would agree with Vincent Sheean that "the Yangtze now runs through Main Street." And in view of the fabulous changes of the past 160 years, I think that Washington would likewise endorse the late Henry L. Stimson's dictum that "foreign policy has become our primary domestic concern."

No nation can be "an island unto itself" in this compacted world of the twentieth century's second half. To live and to work with a sense of world community is the wellspring of our way and will for peace.

It is this sense of interdependence among peoples that has given the word politics a new meaning for me. I am convinced that if we are going to continue to have Republican and Democratic parties and free elections rather than the one-party, one-candidate system of the garrison state we have to begin thinking, as never before, in terms of world politics. Actually, world politics shapes our lives more tellingly than ward politics. A coffee blight in Brazil, a famine in India, devaluation in Britain, the almost perpetual cabinet crises in France, the discovery of uranium ore in Africa, a political assassination in Lebanon, all have an increasingly direct and pervasive influence upon decisions which determine our destiny as individuals and as a people. It seems to me that we all must agree with the editors of *Barron's* when they affirm that "every nation in the world, past and present, has had to learn at one point or another . . . of the supremacy of foreign over domestic affairs. The latter, it is true, are very . . . visible and immediate in their impact, and for that reason absorb a large part of public attention. However, the really decisive events, although their effect is often delayed, are almost always those of relationships with other nations. It is foreign policy which makes history."

What all of this means is that world politics is a vital salient in waging the peace, and that we must have a foreign policy in time of peace which is quite as positive as foreign policy in time of war. Yet it has been only within the past decade that our peacetime foreign policy has been shifting away from the negative toward the positive. Before reviewing briefly what happened, let us look into the question of who makes foreign policy and who puts it into effect.

Under the Constitution the President makes foreign policy and the State Department carries it out. In practice, however, Congress has a great deal to say. It is the Senate which has to ratify treaties, and both Senate and House can grant or deny funds for any foreign policy purpose. What any branch of the government may do in this area also reflects public opinion in general and the pressures and persuasions of special interest groups in particular. Business associations, labor unions and farm federations all have a hand in molding foreign policy. So, too, do newspaper columnists, radio commentators, educators and ministers. So does everybody else. The fact is that we all make foreign policy, out of our ignorance or out of our knowledge, out of our courage or out of our fear.

Our aim should be a clear, well-defined creative policy that can bring into balance our objectives and our resources. We must take into account what we want to do in relation to what we have to do it with, otherwise we will overreach ourselves and end up with confusion and futility.

While everybody makes foreign policy, the major burden of crystallizing it rests upon the State Department. In coping with this challenge, it is hampered not only by the carry-overs of our ingrained isolationism but also by traditional suspicion of its personnel. I must confess that when I came to Washington I carried around in my own mind quite a few of the customary stereotypes about the State Department. I tended to visualize it in terms of striped trousers and wing collars, the mark of an aloof priesthood which presided over a mystic and elaborate ritualism of something called "protocol." I thought of the State Department as an aggregation of cooky-pushers whose only diploma was the parchment of snobbism signed by family wealth and connections. Certainly they were more concerned with place cards at a formal dinner

118

than with political convulsions in a former dependency.

I found out that nothing could be farther from the truth. During my two and a half years as ECA administrator I learned that the State Department is staffed with extremely hard-working, devoted and competent people. They are drawn from all groups in our society. The very growth of the department from fifty-four hundred in 1939 to some twenty-four thousand today attests not only to the growth in America's world leadership responsibilities but also to the fact that its qualifications are hardly confined to social position and inherited opulence.

Moreover, it has been heartening to see in Washington and elsewhere a growing awareness of State Department accomplishments. It has made a most constructive contribution in helping to brace, to extend and even to invent those international organizations which are today's promises of peace. It did much, for example, to lay the groundwork for the United Nations and to make it an agency for building and enforcing peace. The department has, moreover, worked through various branches of the UN to foster world co-operation, along with good will toward our country and an understanding of our aims. It has worked through the UN's Food and Agricultural Organization to spread knowledge overseas of American methods of soil, seed and livestock improvement, and through the World Health Organization to introduce American techniques of medical care.

It has worked through UNESCO to share American achievements in the realm of the mind and the spirit. To quicken and enlarge the exchange of goods and services among world markets it has, together with other government agencies, helped to sponsor the proposed International Trade Organization as still another UN span in the bridge of world peace.

Even more important, perhaps, the State Department largely developed the Truman Doctrine, the Marshall Plan, the Mutual Defense Assistance Program and the North Atlantic Treaty which, along with our participation in the UN, form the key elements of a positive foreign policy in peacetime. The advantage of a positive policy is undeniable when we contrast our marked success in Western Europe with our lack of success in Asia, where our policy has been less certain. The United States has long since passed the stage when it could afford, in any area of the world, the kind of negative foreign policy that for generations could be summed up by references to Freedom of the Seas, the Monroe Doctrine, the Open Door, Manifest Destiny and the Panama Canal. It was precisely this kind of foreign policy which, in the years after World War I, prompted us to abstain from the League of Nations, to indulge in shortsighted grants and loans to Europe, and to put faith in the resounding and futile phrases of the Kellogg-Briand Pact to "renounce" war.

The need for a positive foreign policy to define our relations with all peoples in all parts of the world is of such surpassing importance that I believe the State Department should concentrate all its energies upon this task. It should do this to the exclusion of everything else, except the diplomatic functions performed by its embassies and legations.

It should, for example, in conjunction with other appropriate branches of government, determine just what areas should receive economic aid or propaganda attention, in light of our over-all political objectives. It should not dilute its energies nor divert its skills from this transcendent task of policy-making by trying to administer a Point Four program or the Voice of America. To engage in these or similar pursuits, instead of delegating them to separate operational agencies, is to confuse staff with line functions.

The advantages of keeping staff and line functions apart have been tested by the Economic Cooperation Administration. ECA was set up as a separate agency to carry out a political aim, a foreign policy directive, by means of an economic aid program. When the ECA was being established, considerable anxiety was expressed lest the State Department and the ECA get embroiled in jurisdictional disputes. Indeed, Congress was so worried about this possibility that it wrote into the Foreign Assistance Act of 1948 (the enabling legislation for ECA) that the ECA administrator and the Secretary of State should "keep each other fully and currently informed" and arrive at mutually acceptable decisions. In case of any moot point which could not be resolved between them, the disagreement was to be laid directly before the President. To date, there has never been a conflict of this kind to take to the President, and I am confident that there will never be one.

Actually, ECA has had the fullest co-operation from the State Department and could not have gone forward successfully without it. I believe that ECA, in turn, by working in the economic field, has helped the State Department move toward one of its major goals: to encourage the peoples of Western Europe to work together more closely than ever before and to perceive more clearly the common character of their problems, their opportunities, and their perils. I submit that recent progress in this direction has been due in part to ECA's drive to foster economic integration. The good thing about the spirit of unity is that it ramifies out; when you cultivate habits of unity in the economic sphere, they naturally spread over to the political sphere and even to the military sphere when the need arises.

As I can testify from my own experience, the potentials for this unity exist. When I made my first visit to Europe as ECA administrator, back in July 1948, I saw that Western Europe's economy then was like a crazy quilt whose varicolored squares had been cut out but not sewn together. Each nation was striving to be self-sufficient. With this as a goal no single country, nor all sixteen of them individually, could possibly make substantial use of the Continent's resources. For fifty years, indeed, Western Europe had been moving in the direction of economic nationalism. Countries competed with each other in intensifying trade restrictions, in raising tariffs and in imposing import quotas and exchange controls to "protect" home industries which were uneconomic and old-fashioned. These impediments to trade naturally made matters worse. They hindered Europe from taking advantage of modern techniques of large-scale, low-cost production which, during those same fifty years, largely accounted for the higher productivity of United States industry and the higher living standards of the American people. The reason is very simple. Large-scale, low-cost production is possible only in a sizable, unified and unrestricted market area where goods can move freely from factory to consumer.

The harm done by trade barriers among the European nations is best illustrated by comparative production figures between Europe and the United States. In 1900 the per capita output of the European worker and the American worker was virtually the same. Both lived on about the same scale. Yet in 1950 the United States, with a population of 151,000,000, turned out a gross

123

national product of $279,000,000,000 in contrast to
the Marshall Plan countries which, with 274,000,000
people, turned out a gross national product of only $170,-
000,000,000. If, however, European per capita output
had been on a par with ours, their gross national product
would have been around $500,000,000,000. Of course
Western Europe lacks both the raw materials and the
horsepower for this rate of production. Its application of
the industrial arts will lag behind ours for an indefinite
time. Yet a free-trading European market, unhampered
by tariffs and controls, might well have enabled Western
Europe to achieve $100,000,000,000 more production.
That extra $100,000,000,000 would have made it far
easier for Marshall Plan nations to move both toward
higher prosperity and faster rearmament.

From the outset, of course, our interest in reducing
trade barriers among Western Europe's peoples had more
than an economic motivation. We never forgot for a
moment that the Marshall Plan is a program for peace
and that economic *autarchy* and attempts to attain it
often have been the basis for strife. We believed, for
example, that Hitler might never have had the final impetus to start World War II if it had not been for the
self-sufficiency fence he threw around Germany. It was
this fence which largely enabled him to build up, for the
sole purpose of waging war, synthetic fuel, synthetic
rubber and new steel plants, all at excessively high cost,

all unable to withstand competition from outside Germany.

Obviously, the greatest single contribution the ECA could make to Europe's enduring prosperity was to help it toward economic integration. I wish I could say that this has been done, that as a result of ECA activities all sections of the European economy have been welded into a single market as unencumbered by trade impediments as our own American market. Unfortunately, that is not true. Europe is still plagued with tariffs which slow down the exchange of goods and services among the countries. Nevertheless, enough progress has been made to enable me to say definitely that the trend toward autarchy has been reversed.

Trade among the European countries, which had been reduced almost to the vanishing point, was set in motion again during the first year of the Marshall Plan by an ECA-financed payments plan. This enabled European producers to get dollars for goods shipped in intra-European trade. It was the only device that could be used in view of the fact that the value placed on currencies by many governments was completely out of line with their value in the free market. During this same period the participating countries also agreed to remove from their respective import control lists some 50 per cent of the items in intra-European trade.

It was the devaluation of the British pound which

gave us the opportunity to clear a new path through the tangled undergrowth of intra-European trade. Devaluation prompted revaluation of virtually all European currencies, and it was this reshuffling process that provided the opening we had long sought; namely, to bring into being a European Payments Union to make francs, lire, guilders and pounds freely convertible in the intra-European market. This means, in effect, that each participant can use the proceeds from exports to one country to pay for imports from another. At the same time, as part of the agreement which set up the Payments Union, quantitative restrictions were removed from an additional 10 per cent of the commodities. Thus 60 per cent of private intra-European trade in foodstuffs, raw materials and manufactured goods became free; and the goal of 75 per cent trade liberalization will be reached in the near future.

The European Payments Union illustrates again the inseparable and reciprocal character of the political and economic in these days. Chancellery and parliament, as well as industry and agriculture, had a hand in developing the European Payments Union, which affects the livelihoods of 274,000,000 people.

I wish that I had the space and the eloquence to tell the full story of the European Payments Union, the creative vision it represents, the delicate and complex negotiations that made it a reality, the subordination of short-term national interest to long-term supra-national interest that went into its making. But I have to content myself with pointing out that it is a going concern, that it operates under ECA guidance as a jointly financed venture which combines the features of the old gold standard, a credit clearinghouse and a constant dispenser of inter-European good will and good faith.

It was this new atmosphere of mutuality which made it possible for the Schuman Plan to be born. The Schuman Plan is designed to pool the coal and iron resources of Western Europe, from mine to strip mill to point of sale, and it also underscores the connection between the political and economic. In setting forth this proposal, the Quai d'Orsay declared: "Europe will not be built at one stroke, nor by a frontal attack on the whole problem at one and the same time. It will grow out of concrete achievements that will make solidarity an actual fact. . . . In order to bring together the nations of Europe, the centuries-old hostility between France and Germany must cease to exist. . . . By pooling raw materials and setting up a high authority, whose decision would be binding on France, Germany and the other member countries, this proposal would lay the first real foundations of a European Federation, which is essential to the preservation of peace. . . ." These political aims of the Schuman Plan are to be served by its economic objectives: to supply coal and steel on equal terms in the markets of all member countries; to modernize output, improve quality, raise labor's living standards and earn higher profits for ownership.

The very idea of the Schuman Plan would have been unthinkable a generation ago. Yet at the very time this book is going to press, spokesmen for the governments of France, Western Germany, Italy, the Netherlands, Belgium and Luxembourg are preparing to sign the Schuman Plan Treaty. Its political aims are bold and far-reaching enough to become steppingstones toward that European Federation which many believe is the next necessary step in Western Europe's political evolution. The new array of supra-national authorities set up under the Schuman Plan will be empowered to abolish not only national trade barriers but also private restrictive agreements. This approach should be compared to that behind the formation of the European steel cartel in the 1920s, under which producers and sellers divided markets, rigidly "pegged" and protected prices and held back production.

Far from promoting efficiency or easing trade impediments, the cartel froze Western Europe's steel industry into a carked mold, a major reason why the industry has been ossified until Marshall Plan influences have brought it up to date in terms of technology and a concerted drive toward a single market, flexible prices and better wage and working conditions. The Schuman

Plan, in short, is an anti-cartel plan to fuse and expand, rather than to divide and constrict, the coal and steel resources of Western Europe. I believe that the Schuman Plan demonstrates that the most important and lasting benefits from all such advances on the economic front will be found in the impetus and inspiration they are giving to Western Europeans to duplicate, in the political and defense areas, the same kind of co-operation and integration that they are achieving in economic affairs.

I believe that the supreme political significance of the ECA is that it has developed techniques of collaboration under which a powerful nation like the United States can establish an effective working partnership with a less powerful nation, without exacting from the latter any surrender of the right to rule itself. The ECA is, therefore, the first major experiment in the history of world politics where a strong power, while participating in the internal affairs of a weaker one, has not only refused to infringe upon freedom of choice, but rather invoked every means to conserve that freedom. This experience is proving to be of great value in the Philippines, Indonesia and Burma where newly independent nations are hypersensitive to any suggestion of control or domination.

Despite the natural American urgency to achieve efficiency, ECA personnel, when faced with the choice between efficiency and freedom, always chooses freedom, a point which was emphasized by the *London Economist*. The determination to achieve Western European recovery has been throughout an act of self-determination in the best meaning of Woodrow Wilson's use of that term.

What gives me greatest pride in all my association with the ECA is that it has consistently confirmed the principle that the only way to make democracy work is to work through the ways of democracy. This means the ability to chart a middle course between extremes, to find accommodation between opposing interests and to do these things not by ukase nor by threat of force, but by means of discussion and debate. I have always felt that the conference table is the most unappreciated weapon in the arsenal of democracy. I am always moved when I think of how quietly and effectively ECA personnel overseas has exemplified this kind of political maturity which is simply respect for the dignity, the opinions and the concerns of others. I feel that this pattern of conduct gave the real meaning to our exports of food and machinery. And I am sure that our national experience in easing frictions among ourselves, the whole give-and-take flexibility which is the essence of our domestic politics, has provided us with an invaluable apprenticeship for our newer tasks in world politics.

We have learned in Europe what to do in Asia, for under the Marshall Plan, we have developed the essential instruments of a successful policy in the arena of world politics. While in Europe we concentrated on turbines and tractors, in Asia we are primarily concerned with vaccines and fertilizers. But the political principle remains the same. Only the deeds of democracy can enable the peoples still undecided between the lures of despotism and the life of freedom to make an honest choice.

Certainly I want nothing I have said to convey the impression that we have as yet all the answers when it comes to waging the peace along the political front. We could not have, for we have begun to pursue a positive foreign policy too recently to do anything more than devise vanguard operations in some places and to ask the right questions about other places. Our position of world leadership is still new to us, and we are still in the process of determining and rounding out a positive foreign policy for waging the peace and deciding what agencies we need to carry it out. I believe that in the Congress and in the Executive and among our people generally there is a growing recognition of how urgent and how crucial it is for us to get our backs into this job. I feel, of course, that we have not much choice about it. Either we do it and do it efficiently or we perish, for the danger is clear and present and the hour is late.

CHAPTER 8

Waging the Peace on the Information Front

Much of my life has been spent developing products, studying markets and determining how best to persuade people to buy my company's wares. I always proceeded on one assumption: that the product had to be good to retain a market. On the basis of that assumption, I was not for many years too concerned about Communism. As a political theory, it seemed reactionary to me rather than progressive; and as put into practice by the Kremlin, it had yoked the Russian people to a new stream-lined terror in place of an old-fashioned tyranny. I simply could not believe that it could continue to hold its market at home, let alone gain new markets abroad.

I was rudely awakened from my complacency when I visited Europe in the fall of 1946. I came face to face with the fact that millions of people in Italy, France and Western Germany were convinced that Communism offered them a better way of life than democracy. I recognized, of course, that this was in large measure due to the desperate plight in which most of these people found themselves at the end of World War II. Communist barkers were exploiting their misery, decoying them with the promise that only when their countries had gone Communist could they have bread for their hunger and security instead of want. This spiel was used with telling effect among the poor. However, destitution alone did not fully explain Communism's appeal, for among those embracing this creed were many intellectuals and other professional groups and even men of substantial wealth. As I explored further I discovered that Soviet success in Western Europe derived in large part from a Communist propaganda incredibly adroit, incessant, and tailored to the prejudices and emotions of people in all walks of life.

The special peril of Communist propaganda is that it exploits for selfish purposes the deep human yearnings for co-operation and freedom. It lays claim to the very phrases of Christian ethics, of brotherhood and of peace, to mask practices of barbarism, perfidy and war. In comparison with the sleight-of-hand practitioners of Communist propaganda who confuse and warp men's minds, Goebbels was a neophyte and Machiavelli an amateur. As I realized this shocking fact it became painfully obvious to me that if the free world was to thrust back Communism it would not only have to improve living conditions, especially for the underprivileged, but would also have to counter the Kremlin's propaganda of the lie with its own propaganda of the truth.

To many Americans, of course, the very word propaganda is suspect and even evil. It has become associated in our thinking with deceit and trickery, with totalitarian rather than democratic methods. As employed by Hitler and Stalin, it has become the synonym for the Big Lie. Yet propaganda need not be these things. The word originally meant to propagate an idea or a faith. From the standpoint of this original meaning, it can be used to serve creative and moral as well as destructive and amoral ends. We must, I believe, start thinking of propaganda in these terms. I realize that in Congress and among our people generally a tremendous amount of confusion persists between "propaganda" and "information" functions. To distinguish between them, I commend the definition developed by Mr. Lester Markel, Sunday editor of the New York *Times*. He points out that the two terms are used as if they were direct opposites, but that the difference between them is not always clear cut and simple. That difference, he suggests, might broadly be put this way:

"Information is the communication of facts and opinions in an effort to *enlighten*.

"Propaganda is the communication of facts (or nonfacts) and opinions in an effort to *influence*.

"Information, presumably, is calm, coldly logical, un-emotional; propaganda is turbulent, hotly persuasive, supercharged with emotion. But the distinction is not that easy," he continues. "On the one hand, propaganda may be the utterly calm presentation of lies. On the other hand, facts set down coldly and objectively often have a greater influence than flaming unfactual words."

Even though the boundary line between propaganda and information may be at times obscured, says Mr. Markel, we would do well to recognize that in today's contest for men's heads and hearts America has two principal tasks.

1. At home here, we must give our people the facts and reasons behind everything that we do in the sphere of foreign policy to enable them to understand its aims. This is an *information* job, since it is an attempt to enlighten.

2. Overseas, we must make doubly sure that we are understood by other peoples, that our aims are set forth clearly and forthrightly in a way to advance our case and our cause. This is a *propaganda* job, since it is an attempt to influence and to convince.

In the area of seeking to influence and convince, the men of the Kremlin are immeasurably aided by something we have not yet crystallized to a sufficient extent: a body of doctrine, a product to sell.

This body of doctrine originated in the studies of

Marx and Engels, who envisioned a classless society in which the state "withers away" and men live in peace and brotherhood. The fact that the theories of Marx and Engels, as they have been put into practice by Lenin and Stalin, have brought into being a dictatorship in which an elite group rules with brutality and ruthlessness has not prevented the use of the theoretical Marxist doctrine for propaganda purposes.

To disseminate this doctrine, the men of the Kremlin have organized a vast apparatus. It is skillfully manned and heavily financed. It is used to achieve and maintain "thought control" of both Soviet and satellite peoples as well as for external propaganda designed to pervert the thinking of free peoples. It is a major instrument of Kremlin policy and as such is directed by the potent Department of Agitation and Propaganda of the Communist Party. Both Lenin and Stalin have given meticulous attention to perfecting its program and techniques.

Let us take a look at the operation of this apparatus in just one country, France, where the Kremlin has made one of its strongest bids for conquest by internal aggression.

In France, which has less than one-third the population of the United States, the Communist party is roughly ten times the size of its American counterpart. Best present estimates of the number of hard-core, active, completely dedicated Communist party militants run up to 250,000 out of a card carrying membership of between 600,000 and 700,000. These form the disciplined center which day and night, year in and year out, preaches the Kremlin gospel. The French Communist party like Communist parties everywhere else is primarily an instrument of Soviet foreign policy, under the absolute control of the Kremlin.

On the basis of a carefully planned strategy, the Communists attempt to capitalize on grievances in every section of French society and drive wedges between the sections. They sponsor women's organizations and clubs for war veterans, former resistance members, bombed-out families, war widows, deportees and former prisoners of war. The Communists also work through and upon tenant groups, family associations and sporting fraternities—even bowling and fishermen's clubs. And perilously close to the late George Orwell's nightmare vision of *Nineteen Eighty-four* is a new and very present human horror: the tale-bearing, key-carrying, mail-snooping *concierge*. She is supposed to be the guardian of the home and its privacy. But many *concierges* have been organized and venomized as informers by the Communist party to act as sources of blackmail against those who oppose it. Such instruments and agents of the world's current Inquisition, along with various "front" organizations, more or less camouflaged, have grown up like chokeweeds in French life.

The Communists control the General Confederation of Labor (CGT), the largest trade-union organization in France. It has lost some of its strength in the past two years, but it still has some 2,250,000 members, most of them in industries of strategic economic and military importance. Although the CGT is Communist-led, the rank-and-file membership is far from 100 per cent Communist. Exactly what percentage belongs to the party is not known, but the furor raised by the labor press is very well known.

And the press, in general, is the most powerful Communist outlet in France. There are Communist dailies, weeklies, monthlies. There is a special publication for every influential group—for farmers, for intellectuals, for maritime workers, for ministers, for young people, for women, for Parisians. There is a special Communist publication for every region—often for every little town. There are Communist papers for Alsace-Lorraine in German, special editions for the Mediterranean coast and for the mountain regions near Grenoble. There are large Communist daily newspapers, picture magazines, political tracts and sensational scandal sheets. Possibly the most important weapon of all is the recently established Communist press association, L'Union d'Information Française. This wire service co-ordinates the Communist press network. At a moment's notice the nation can be blanketed with any given story.

Since many Communist publications are disguised, it is difficult to catalogue them all. They range in audience appeal from dressmaking to football scores. There are more than a hundred of such publications and at least forty of them in Paris alone. They all feature pro-Communist, anti-American, anti-Marshall Plan propaganda. In addition, there are speeches, meetings and direct personal appeals. There are peace rallies, birthday celebrations and union picnics. Communist posters shout at Frenchmen from every vacant wall, in subway stations and even in cafés. There are Communist books, films and lecture tours. The devices are almost endless.

While some revenue sources of the French Communist party are known, many are not, and there is little doubt that this unattributed difference is filled by the Kremlin. A very conservative estimate indicates that the Communist party of France spends five to six billion francs a year, or from fifteen to seventeen million dollars, to carry out its program.

It is this kind of all-embracing propaganda, carefully conceived, devoutly executed and impeccably timed, which confronts the free world.

How, then, can the free world unmask the claims of Communist propaganda and liberate the minds it has enchained?

First we must crystallize a free world doctrine which reflects the ideals and strivings of free men around the globe. Then we must find words with which to express this doctrine, words that will, as Kipling put it, "walk up and down in the hearts of men."

I am sure we can draw up this free world doctrine to reinspire those who take freedom too much for granted, and even win the loyalty of those now cringing in serfdom. To set forth this doctrine is merely to spell out for today's world the terms of our legacy. We are, after all, the inheritors of Magna Carta and the Declaration of Independence, which in turn drew upon the principles set forth by Confucius, by Plato and pre-eminently by Christ in His Sermon on the Mount. Our free world doctrine should cover four major fields:

RELIGIOUS—in terms of freedom of worship, the worth of the individual and the brotherhood of man;

POLITICAL—not in forms of government, but in the charter of civil liberties which drafters of the United States Constitution distilled from the accumulated experience of the Western world;

ECONOMIC—in terms of the new, socially conscious capitalism which, in the United States, has been developed to an extent which the world as a whole little understands; a system based on widespread ownership, diffusion of initiative, decision and enterprise and an ever-widening distribution of its benefits;

SOCIAL—in the sense of that humanism which leads us to search for both public and private instruments that will increasingly equalize and expand opportunity—economic, educational and cultural; media that will further safeguard the individual against life's common hazards, whether this protection takes the form of the International Red Cross, Social Security laws or industry's pension programs.

Once our free world doctrine is defined, the second step is to propagate it as widely as possible—by every means.

Here again we must remember that the United States can help others to help themselves. But it cannot and should not try to do the job by itself alone. The doctrine will have far greater appeal if it is, to every extent possible, presented in each country by its own nationals. This is as equally true for free countries as for those behind the Iron Curtain. Frenchmen will be much more effective than Americans in getting their compatriots, whether on the extreme left or extreme right, to embrace the doctrine of freedom. Similarly, Poles operating within Poland or outside will be much more successful than anyone else in keeping alive and vibrant the quest for freedom among Polish people.

The United States, however, does have immense responsibilities for propaganda beyond its own borders. As the leader of the free world, it must by deeds and words make clear to all peoples our devotion to the ideal of a free, peaceful and more ample life for all men.

Ours in a new sense must be a propaganda of the deed, of visible accomplishments. Our deeds under the Marshall Plan in Europe, our current program in Southeast Asia and Point Four are the most convincing techniques we can have. But these deeds must be rounded out by a well-co-ordinated propaganda, imaginative alike in the variety of its projects and in the vigor of its impact.

I indicated in a previous chapter something of what confronted us when the Cominform was leveled at the Marshall Plan. Of course we had our doctrine already formed for us in the Marshall Plan itself—an obviously constructive plan aimed at restoring Europe to strength and self-reliance, a commendable effort under any definition. But we lacked the means to tell our story.

We had originally believed that in ECA we would require very little informational apparatus. Indeed, we thought in terms of a man or two in each of the ECA missions overseas to get out press releases, contact local editors and to report back home on progress. We soon learned that the Communists outnumbered us on this front about fifty to one. We also quickly learned that something more potent than the mimeograph machine was required to get our story told, our product sold.

We recruited talent from the top American newspapers, magazines, radio networks and movie concerns. As we built up our staff under the able and dynamic Bob

Mullen in Washington and the resourceful Roscoe Drummond in Paris we increased our budget for this purpose, with the strong support of Congress, from about $2,000,000 to almost $17,000,000 in counterpart funds.

The Marshall Plan Mobile Exhibit which helped make millions of Europeans aware of the Marshall Plan illustrates, for example, the sort of project which our propaganda program could everywhere include. Called "Europe Builds," this self-contained Marshall Plan exhibit is now on a 6,000-mile tour of Western European countries. It carries its own tent, runs its own motion pictures, features its own puppet shows, all in the languages of the different countries. It has already been shown in France, Belgium, Denmark, Germany and Sweden. It tells the story of progress toward Western integration and what this will mean in terms of higher living standards and a more secure peace when 274,-000,000 Europeans can produce for each other and sell to each other more freely.

An effective feature of the "Europe Builds" exhibit has been the half million toy balloons it has released into the still free air. Brightly colored, hydrogen-filled, about one foot in diameter, each one has carried a post card with a return address signed by the person who sends it up. It is a greeting of friendship and good will from one European to another. When the Marshall Plan caravan was in Denmark, about seventy thousand balloons were released, each carrying a message which read in part:

WITH THIS BALLOON you receive a sincere greeting from a peace-loving friend in Denmark who has visited the Marshall Plan exhibition "Europe Builds" at Copenhagen.

The balloon is a symbol of the hopes for peace and prosperity entertained by the free, democratic citizens of the 18 Marshall Plan countries. It is a symbol of the free exchange of goods and ideas that all of us attempt to realize. Our hope is that one day people and goods will be able to pass the borders as freely as the balloons can move over land and sea.

The Marshall Plan—a plan for democratic peace.

Some balloons floated two hundred, three hundred, five hundred miles away, and then they dropped silently in East Germany, in Poland and in Hungary; in Austria; in Czechoslovakia and in Lithuania.

A few wisps of truth had blown over the top of the Iron Curtain, and this is how the Communists reacted:

1. Government spokesmen warned that it was physically dangerous to pick up the balloons and the messages they carried; they might explode.

2. Those who turned them over to the police were publicly commended.

3. The Communist press and radio began a strident campaign of anti-American accusations charging that "Western imperialists attached dangerous microbes to

the printed messages," and asserting that the purpose of the balloons was to study "air currents prior to launching bacteriological warfare against Europe."

There were other reactions from behind the Iron Curtain. Somehow letters from Hungarians, Poles and others reached friends outside the Iron Curtain and were relayed to ECA missions.

"I want to send you this in a secret way," some wrote. A typical note said, "Your balloon has blown a long way. It has blown to a part of Europe where people do not speak—or rather dare not speak—about the ideas you support and work for. But we are longing very much for the day when we can live as Europeans. Don't think that Europe ends at the Iron Curtain." Other letters told nearly the same story, a story of frustration and fear, tempered by hope.

From this, and from dozens of other results of our Marshall Plan informational efforts, to say nothing of businesslike public-opinion surveys which we had made by outside concerns, I am convinced that the majority of people in Europe ardently stand with us, and that those in the satellite states are eager to know what is happening in the free world.

As our third step in meeting the heavy responsibilities the United States must carry in this field of propaganda, we must unify decisively and fully our government's information activities just as we have begun to unify our defense forces. We must create a single independent Overseas Information Agency and give it clear-cut authority. This agency should be headed by an administrator with cabinet status. This is no "left-handed" job for any agency or department of government with other pursuits as its first concern. Nor is it a job to be directed by an assistant secretary of anything.

If we see this propaganda program for what I think it should be—and what our opponents have made it—namely, a major instrument of national policy, then we must give it the standing and support it deserves. By doing so we should first rid ourselves of some of the overlapping operations we now have in this field as between, for example, the Marshall Plan information program and the United States Information Service of the Department of State.

We should abolish some of the hampering restrictions now placed upon our information specialists by policy formulations in which they have no voice, by delays in getting decisions from men overburdened with other duties and unfamiliar with propaganda techniques and their timing.

Most of all, by placing this means of waging the peace at the highest policy-making level we would attract to its service men of exceptional ability and drive. We need men who can use all the tools of propaganda with imagination, boldness and skill, tempered by a judgment which derives from a sensitive awareness of the forces of world ferment.

We shall have to sharpen our understanding of the kind of men best fitted for this work in the same way that we must sharpen our understanding of the difference between propaganda, news reporting or broadcasting, information, publicity, advertising and other related fields of communication.

The born propagandist is difficult to identify by any formal symbols. He is not necessarily, for instance, a man with newspaper training, although he may be, as was the late Charles Michelson.

He is most likely to be a man who knows something of all the methods and media of mass communication and how to orchestrate them. But he must also think in terms of the deed which generates its own propaganda and how to bring it about, and he knows the power of individual word-of-mouth communication to support more formalized techniques. The propagandist is not satisfied to inform—he seeks to persuade. He is a trial lawyer, seeking a verdict at the bar of public opinion. Once the importance of his role is recognized he can plan to extract the utmost in psychological benefits from foreign policy and action as these unfold.

Arguments are sometimes advanced that no formal government agency, under a political system such as ours, can ever effectively combat the Communist propaganda apparatus. Admittedly, any government agency under our zealously guarded freedom of speech will be subject to some handicaps not met by either a non-governmental agency or the agency of a dictatorship.

The fact remains, however, that the sums required for this task must come primarily from appropriations made by the Congress, and any agency expending them must therefore ultimately report to the Congress and be responsible to it. My experience as ECA administrator has convinced me that the opportunities for effective administration are just as great through a straightforward government agency as they are through any other device, such as a government-financed corporation.

Fourth, we need a creative approach to the propaganda task. We need, in particular, to recognize how little is yet known of the art of communication—and especially of communication between people such as ourselves and others whose heritage has made them different from ourselves.

Hence, we need in our propaganda operation a continuing program of research and testing, just as our military forces need it in theirs. We must work with the tools we have—which we are not yet fully doing—and we must also seek to improve them and devise better ones.

Fifth, we need—once we have more sharply defined our responsibilities—to step up the volume of our propaganda, which means spending a great deal more money than we are doing now.

Our present appropriations for our major national effort in this field, through the Department of State, total $120,000,000. Even this sum was authorized only after strenuous efforts by such people as Senator William Benton (D., Conn.), and marked a substantial increase over preceding ones. But this sum is only a tiny fraction of the propaganda funds matched against us by the Kremlin-controlled Communist parties of the world.

From what I have seen of the beneficial ways in which propaganda money can be used for the Marshall Plan in Western Europe alone, I know that this sum is wholly inadequate for our world-wide needs. We should be prepared to step up these expenditures to at least $300,000,000, or perhaps even more, as rapidly as their effective use can be demonstrated. For the battle to win a country through the minds, hearts and loyalties of its people will always be an infinitely cheaper battle than that which has to be won by armies—as the Kremlin has so spectacularly proven.

In appropriating this money we need to have at least 15 per cent of it on a confidential basis, free from the need of public disclosure and usable at the discretion of the administrator. The most successful propaganda means are not always conventional, not always foreseeable and not always those which move within a gold-fish bowl. Unless we equip our directors of propaganda with the funds to use non-public methods as they may be required, we seriously handicap them. We can give them this necessary freedom of maneuver and provide sufficient safeguards through auditing by the General Accounting Office and private reporting to the committees of the Congress.

Sixth, we need to inspire and promote and, if necessary, help finance a non-governmental crusading propaganda agency to supplement the work of the proposed government agency and to do some of the things that are outside the province of government.

Such an agency should be broad enough to become world-wide in scope with organized, affiliated forces in as many countries as possible. It should seek to enlist millions of average men and women under its banners, for its financial support and in a crusade for the free world doctrine. It should thus answer the "What can I do?" question which millions of still free men and women are asking.

This non-governmental agency should undertake two major functions. First, it should seek to supply, organize, train and direct a nucleus of oral missionaries who will carry the doctrine of the free world into every village, neighborhood, shop, farm community, union hall or other group.

This is a huge job, a difficult and even a dangerous job, and it must be accomplished largely on a basis of voluntary enlistment, of genuine dedication. Yet anyone who has studied the methodology of the Kremlin in this field and seen at first hand the evidence of its effectiveness will know that this is a task we will ignore at very great risk indeed. To be without such a free world force for freedom working with and for us in this effort is like launching an advertising campaign without a sales staff, or a political campaign without precinct workers to ring doorbells.

The second major task which this non-governmental agency should undertake is a sustained propaganda offensive to destroy the credibility of the Communist doctrine, to show time and again that its promises are not fulfilled.

We have barely tapped the possibilities which stem from the Kremlin's reliance on the Big Lie. This is the Kremlin's most vulnerable spot. Its whole doctrine is erected on a *misinterpretation* of history. Its very flag, with its symbolism of peasant and worker control of the state, is a lie. Its "classless society" has produced sharply differentiated classes. Its political twistings and turnings have produced all the contradictions inherent in a philosophy where the "holy" end justifies the unholy means. Its "freedoms" produce regimentation and its "peace" produces war.

Thus out of their own mouths and acts there is a material, inexhaustible material, for convicting the men of the Kremlin of the Big Lie. By reiteration we can make it stick at all levels, from the intelligentsia to the peasant. We should add to this conviction the relatively untapped power of world ridicule. Wit and humor should be brought to bear on Uncle Joe and his comrades, and the Poor Boob who believes the Kremlin lies should become a familiar figure in every land and language.

I am convinced that in this way the Soviet Communists can be decisively thrown on the defensive and kept so busy answering the truth and trying to suppress it in their own front yard that they will have less time and fewer means to stir up trouble elsewhere.

The peoples of Eastern Europe are beginning to see how much greener the grass is in Western Europe, thanks in large part to the Marshall Plan, which Moscow prevented them from joining. They know that their neighbors are both more prosperous and free. Many of them have heard, too, that the Communists lost virtually every election held in Western Europe after the Marshall Plan began operations.

The peoples of Asia, especially the free peoples, are increasingly aware that the Kremlin's real aim is neither to help the underprivileged nor to liberate colonial peoples, but rather to enslave them and everyone else under

153

Soviet imperialism. The naked aggression of the North Koreans and the unprovoked invasion of the Red Chinese Army, both acting under orders from Moscow have made Kremlin intentions doubly clear.

The free peoples must take their message of freedom and hope over, under, through and around the Iron Curtain in Europe and the Bamboo Curtain in Asia.

We who have worked in the Marshall Plan have found a real and growing response to our information efforts. There is no telling what a sustained, full-scale crusade to propagandize the free world doctrine will do. The evidence is that it will give new hope and determination to those who want freedom and bring new defeats to the enemies of freedom.

The time to start this new and intensified program of free world propaganda is now, if the free world is to be made as invincible in its credo as in its cause.

CHAPTER 9

The Cost of Waging the Peace

On May 8, 1950, I was slated to speak before a convention of the Kiwanis International in Miami, Florida. I was looking forward eagerly not only to telling the ECA story to the Kiwanians but to a reunion with my good friend Captain Eddie Rickenbacker, who was also on the program. I had known him for a long time. When I was selling Studebakers in Los Angeles before World War I, he was the fair-haired boy in the Mercer Agency, much envied, I might add, by all of us on automobile row as he dashed about demonstrating the Mercer Sport Roadster, a great car in its day.

However, the Senate Appropriations Committee scheduled its ECA hearings in May and I had to stay in Washington. When I picked up my newspaper on Tuesday morning, May 9, I was startled by a report on Captain Rickenbacker's speech, in which he was quoted as saying that a Marshall Plan for the world would cost $200,000,000,000. He did not actually say quite that, for included in his figure was the cost of rearming the United States. He also said that if the expenditure of $200,000,000,000 could produce peace it would be a bargain. However, the net result of his statement was further confusion as to the cost of foreign aid.

No one can forecast too accurately the cost of waging the peace, but I am willing to make an estimate and put it on the record. Before doing so I should like to repeat that no one in his right senses is thinking of an all-embracing Marshall Plan for the world. However, many men of good sense in many countries are thinking in terms of strengthening those areas vital to the security of the free world. Here is my annual estimate:

Economic aid to those countries in the world whose development is important to the security of the United States and the free world	$2,000,000,000
Political activities	350,000,000
Information activities and propaganda	300,000,000
Unforeseen economic activities	300,000,000
Total	$2,950,000,000

In this estimate I have allowed a cushion of $300,-000,000. At the present time our diplomatic and political activities are costing under $150,000,000 a year, our informational activities under $200,000,000. I am allowing for an expansion on these fronts of $300,000,000. The remaining $300,000,000 is to allow for an expansion of economic activities that cannot now be foreseen.

My estimate for economic aid may seem low in view of what has been spent on the Marshall Plan alone: $6,100,000,000 for the first fifteen months, $3,800,-000,000 for the second year and $2,250,000,000 appropriated for the fiscal year 1951. The explanation, however, is quite simple. My own guess is that out of the thirteen billion dollars that the Marshall Plan will probably cost for the full four years of our program to rebuild and invigorate the economies of Western Europe, some nine billion dollars will have been used for emergency measures of relief and rehabilitation deriving directly from the war itself. This latter sum will have gone for food and medicine; to repair and re-equip railroads and harbors and plants damaged by bombs. That nine billion will not have to be spent again. Only four billion dollars will have been spent to energize the economies of the Marshall Plan countries. In other words, not more than one-third of our Marshall Plan expenditures will have covered the normal postwar needs of economic expansion.

Another reason why economic aid can be held within the figures I have cited is that ECA operations are now expanding only in Southeast Asia. When the economic programs for Indonesia, Indo-China, Burma and Thailand were first proposed, our friends the isolationists let loose anew their characteristic howls of anguish. This meant the outlay of more billions, they charged. Actually, the total cost of the first year's program for all of these countries is estimated at about $84,000,000, and a large part of that $84,000,000 is coming out of savings from the original $275,000,000 appropriation for China. To the $84,000,000 should be added the amounts to be allocated to the Philippines.

There are good reasons—aside from better earnings from exports such as rubber and tin—why this first year's program in Southeast Asia requires this relatively small sum. Southeast Asia is a largely agricultural community and will remain so for many years. The emphasis, therefore, is on agricultural development; on shifting from wooden to steel plows, on better seed and irrigation and soil care. In some areas we will use the techniques we found so effective with the rural rehabilitation program in China. In other areas, however, we must first fight debilitating diseases before we can even begin to help modernize agricultural methods. In Viet Nam (one of the three Associated States of Indo-China), for instance, the great problem is malaria. This must be eradicated, since healthy man power is the first step toward increasing agricultural production. Thus our top-priority project there falls into the health and sanitation field.

Looking ahead in Asia, we must also extend aid not only to India but also to the non-Communist China of the future.

To wage the peace and win it is an aim that so transcends any other reason for investment in the recovery of other nations that only with some hesitation do I suggest it is to our commercial as well as to our political advantage to strengthen the free world. Every businessman knows how difficult it is to build a profitable business in a community that is broke. Obviously, a free world that is steadily growing in prosperity will be a better world in which to do business. Every successful businessman also knows that he must invest a certain amount of his company's annual income to develop markets. Usually that amount ranges from two to five per cent, depending on how much of his advertising program goes into building future, as against current, sales. The sum of $2,950,000,000 which I propose that we invest in waging the peace on the economic, political and informational fronts is around one per cent of our gross national product. Perhaps even from a practical business standpoint that is not too much for a prosperous America to invest in developing world prosperity. If these expenditures help to bring about successful resistance to the Kremlin's internal aggression, they must be regarded as one of the best-paying investments ever made by any people, any time, anywhere.

Compared with the $2,950,000,000 for waging the peace on all three non-military fronts, the $50,000,000,-000 required for waging the peace on the military front looms up as a huge sum. And an annual expenditure of this size will put a strain on our economy that can be lessened only by doing without on the part of our people. Yet if this expenditure deters the Kremlin from external aggression and thus prevents war, we are thoroughly justified in making it and in undergoing the discomforts it entails. A third world war would not only necessitate genuine sacrifice but would also bring individual tragedy and perhaps even national disaster.

How disastrous a third world war would be can best be shown by taking a backward look at World War I and World War II. World War I brought the United States alone 119,000 dead and 194,000 wounded as compared to 306,000 dead and 572,000 wounded in World War II. There is anguish in these cold statistics beyond calculation. Nor can we calculate the cost of the disruption that war brings socially, morally and spiritually.

But we can calculate the cost of the war in dollars. The out-of-pocket cost, or the shooting expense, for World War I was approximately $22,000,000,000; for World War II, approximately $350,000,000,000. I have no data for the ultimate cost of World War I. However, Gordon Gray, ex-Secretary of the Army, reckons that the ultimate cost of World War II, before the last pension is paid, will be approximately one trillion, three hundred billion dollars ($1,300,000,000,000). When I look at that figure, when I note the great increase in the loss of lives in World War II over World War I, when I think of the atom bomb, guided missiles, bacteriological and gas warfare, I find myself overwhelmed by the nightmare vision of what World War III would do to us and everybody else. The prospects of any such catastrophe, if nothing else, should goad us into getting on with waging the peace on all fronts and keeping at it until it is won.

The struggle with the Kremlin may well be long and protracted. It is this prospect which causes me great concern. We are an impatient people, somewhat inclined, even when facing a "long pull," to adopt measures appropriate only to the "short haul." This would be dangerous. It might lead to a different kind of cost, a cost that again cannot be computed in dollars alone—the cost that would result from a lowering of national morale and from a loss of our moral fiber.

In a very real sense, the strength of a nation is a composite of the strength of its individual citizens. We are strong today because our political institutions and economic system have given us as individuals extraordinary opportunity to grow and develop materially and spiritually.

It is this opportunity for growth that has given to American freedom its unique and precious quality. We as a people have enjoyed to a high degree freedom of speech, freedom of worship, freedom from want, freedom from fear. But we also have had, and still have, freedom *for* something—the opportunity to develop our own capacities in an environment that favors energy, initiative and a wide choice of alternatives. This has been the deep source of our strength.

Freedom in this broad sense is not easy to achieve. For a man lives in his community, his country and the world, and he cannot forsake this living and working with other people to go off and search for freedom as an abstract idea. The days of the rugged individualist are over and the days of the co-operative individual are here. The pioneer on his homestead was independent and could go it alone. His descendants, whether at the plow, or loom or desk, whether in village or city, are interdependent. The pioneer forged a free world on his own; his children's children must find their way with all other peoples to a free world.

Freedom can have meaning only when it represents a happy adjustment, a day-to-day and down-to-earth adjustment, of man to man, and men to their society. In today's world we need large-scale complicated arrangements, from collective bargaining to investment banking, to provide the social and economic conditions which assure freedom. And government's role has also become large-scale and complicated—from the National Labor Relations Board to the Securities and Exchange Commission to our more recent Economic Stabilization Board. Whether in normal times or in times of defense preparedness, the government's aim must be to foster those social and economic conditions which assure freedom but without, in the process, taking over so much of the citizen's activities that his energy, his initiative and his choice of alternatives will be undermined.

Ever since the Pilgrims landed at Plymouth Rock and Captain Henry Hudson sailed up the river which bears his name, opportunity for the individual has been a dynamic force in American life. There are those who think it came to a halt at the beginning of this century. I do not agree. I believe a good case can be made for these first fifty years of the twentieth century as the most fruitful in the history of our Republic even while our definition of opportunity has changed with the times.

The most obvious edge the 1951 American has over his grandfather is in the material field. One measure of this lies in the spectacular growth of our gross national product. In 1900 it was $50,000,000,000 in terms of the 1950 dollar; it is now more than five times higher, namely $279,000,000,000, while population has only doubled. Another measure is the spectacular growth in opportunity in both business and the professions. By any yardstick, a nation that had 1,800,000 private enterprises in 1900 and now has 4,000,000 is on the march. In 1920 about 300 laboratories with some 9,000 employees were engaged in industrial research in this country. By 1940 there were 2,200 laboratories with more than 70,000 employees. As for the growth of the national income, today's Americans have more than $136,000,000,000 in savings, an additional $97,100,000,000 in bank deposits and $60,000,000,000 in life insurance policies. As for the rest, I think I need only mention that Americans own 40,000,000 automobiles and 80,000,000 radio sets and let you take it from there.

Our national gains have not stopped with dollars, goods or services by any means. In 1951 most work weeks are down to forty hours. Workmen's compensation laws protect employees against on-the-job injuries. The Social Security Act has set up the federally financed old-age and survivors' insurance program. It also provides for federal-state unemployment insurance to ease the dread of payless shutdowns, along with aid for dependent children, the blind, the totally disabled and the uninsured aged. We have laws prohibiting child labor and laws establishing a minimum wage. Collective bargaining, little known in 1900, is a 1951 commonplace.

Opportunity for our people to grow intellectually and culturally has increased almost as rapidly as opportunity in the material field. Dr. Sumner Slichter of Harvard has said that few periods in the world's history have witnessed such swift advances in breaking down economic barriers to education. Back in 1890, he pointed out, only one out of fourteen children of high school age were still in school; by 1945 the proportion had grown to four out of five. The number of high school graduates has been increasing since 1890 about thirteen times as fast as the population, and the number of college graduates six times as fast. In 1900 we had 7,272 college and university professors; today we have 75,007.

In the sphere of the mind we have been creative; from a James Madison in politics to a William James in psychology to a John Dewey in philosophy. On the purely cultural side we have also done more than to borrow European traditions. "In England," as Lewis Galantière points out, "we see at one end of the cultural spectrum works of American scholarship repeatedly extolled in the learned press and at the other end the deep incrustation of American idioms in English speech. When British provincial newspapers call their biographical sketches 'profiles' and a Labor party rally sings American songs ("The Sidewalks of New York"); when *Punch* takes over from *The New Yorker* its one-line captions and some of its satiric subjects; . . . when a European authority writes that the leading review in the field of aesthetics is that published by the Cleveland Museum of Art—then, clearly, chewing gum, the comics, Coca-

Cola and the tawdrier products of Hollywood cannot be thought of as the only world-wide disseminators of the 'American way of life.'" And as an American let me boast a bit about the recent Nobel Prize award for literature to William Faulkner.

In spiritual growth we may have made the greatest—or the least—gain. Nothing is harder to gauge. But surely our change from a smug indifference to a keen consciousness of the civil rights of others can be assessed as a net advance. The principle of equal opportunity for all which for decades has been neglected has been more recently restored to reflect the aspirations of the Founding Fathers. In my youth it was given lip service but had little reality. To my boys, and to most youngsters of today, civil rights are simply everybody's birthright. In one generation we have come much closer to a working belief in the brotherhood of man. We now increasingly practice what we preach.

In capsule form this is the story of how opportunity to grow materially, culturally and spiritually has increased during the past fifty years. We have the right to be proud of what we have done, but not the right to stop growing. The most exciting fact about America is that it has always been "unfinished business."

We've got to keep it unfinished business and, above all, keep opportunity expanding in the decade of tension that lies ahead. That is not going to be easy. The Kremlin is creating tensions and fears which, unless we are on our guard, will result in actions ill-considered and even hysterical—actions that will constrict the freedom vital to continued growth. Every proposal to curtail either civil liberties or freedom of enterprise must be subjected to a critical examination of its long-term effects.

Everyone recognizes that in order to give priority to our defense efforts some economic controls are necessary. But we should constantly keep in mind that managers produce most when they themselves have the power to make operating decisions and that workers produce best at jobs of their own choosing. Before imposing any control we should make sure that it is imperatively needed and that we make clear our intent to lift it at the end of the emergency that brought it into being.

Even more important than keeping our economy as free as possible is the need to maintain our civil liberties. Loss of liberty is a terrible thing. Still vivid in my mind is the contrast between the people of East and West Berlin. In West Berlin, despite all hardships, the men, the women and children stand upright, and there is hope on their faces. In East Berlin, the people tend to cringe, and if they look at anyone at all, that look is furtive. We can survive this decade of tension in America. We can even expand for ourselves and the whole world continuing opportunities for growth, if we refuse to descend to witch-hunting but instead keep the Bill of Rights as real as today, as up-to-date as tomorrow.

To keep freedom alive at home, to keep our house in order, is to broaden and buttress a base of operations for the effective leadership of the free world. America must now be as eager to grow up as it has been to grow.

There is little doubt that the next ten years will be a time of epic decision, for ourselves and for all men. The choices we make and the risks we run will largely determine the fate of our world for centuries to come. But this prospect, with its problems and its burdens, should not dishearten us. Our nation has faced hardship before and been tempered by it. I cannot but feel that now to fulfill our new responsibilities, far from draining our vitality, will build strength by demanding strength.

CHAPTER 10

Can We Win?

Let us assume that we wage the peace on all fronts with vigor, imagination and dedication; that we do keep our economy strong; that we do accept and affirm our responsibility for the leadership of the free world. What then—what may we expect? Is our best hope that the cold war will be continued, that the Kremlin will intensify its efforts to spread confusion and chaos throughout the free world, and to incite its satellites and puppets to military adventures, while keeping its own Red Army poised and ready to strike? Or can we hope that once we achieve a position of strength we can establish a new balance of power in the world, forcing the Kremlin to live in peace with other nations? Or is there any chance at all that the dictatorial power of the Kremlin may be broken?

These are the questions I have been pondering, and

these are the questions to which I have been trying to get answers from leading statesmen and other authorities both here in America and the world over. I wish I could report a complete unanimity of opinion as to what we may expect, but I cannot, because views differ too widely. The one point, however, on which everyone does agree is that our situation will be vastly improved once we attain a "posture of defense." Winston Churchill, for example, believes that when this has been accomplished we can strike a bargain with the Kremlin, the terms of which it will carry out, provided, as he wryly added, "we maintain our strength." I inferred from what Churchill said that on the diplomatic front the Kremlin functions on a double standard; treaties made with nations whose military might in being they respect are fulfilled—even though grudgingly; treaties made with less powerful nations, or agreements with Soviet appendages, are regarded as mere scraps of paper.

Mr. Churchill was not specific as to precisely what type of bargain we might strike. It may have been his thought that the Kremlin might stop precipitating small localized wars around the globe.

No statesman with whom I talked believed that any genuine change of heart could be expected from the present regime ruling the USSR. Everyone felt that the Politburo is so committed to world conquest that it would never make a trustworthy shift to a policy of "live and let live." That brings us smack up against the chances for a change of regime.

No one believes the present ruling clique will yield to a new faction without tremendous upheaval. Is there, then, any possibility today that it can be pushed out of power? No question is more vital or more sharply debatable. I have good friends and close associates who firmly believe that so tight is the control of the gang at the top, so unassailable is any modern dictatorship from within, that it can collapse only when it has been weakened by attack from without. They point to the ability shown by Hitler and Mussolini to control populations and resources up until their very armies had been defeated and their territories invaded. Moreover, they point out that the Soviet Empire is much larger and stronger than the empires of Hitler and Mussolini; and that its vast land mass contains food and strategic materials that enable it to be largely self-sufficient. It is also further contended that no ruling class has exhibited more sophistication in the use of terror to dominate peoples than the members of the Kremlin hierarchy, and that they have been doing it longer than any other modern dictatorship—including that of Hitler and Mussolini.

Yet I am confident that the downfall of the present regime is inherent in its very structure. That confidence has been fortified by many astute observers, notably John Foster Dulles, General Douglas MacArthur and

George Kennan, along with a number of foreign ministers whose names I cannot disclose.

The exact manner in which the Kremlin's tyranny will be broken is, of course, a matter of conjecture. So is the time. But the tensions that make a breakup likely are concrete and readily discerned.

Many workers in the Soviet Union are restive, resentful and dissatisfied. The Soviet Government failed, after World War II, to fulfill its promise to raise the standard of living. The huge rearmament program absorbed the economic potential that could have gone into improving conditions. Failure to fulfill a promise, especially when it concerns very basic needs, is always dangerous. And those Red Army soldiers who were abroad during World War II remember that Europeans on the western side of the Iron Curtain were far better off.

A vast number of peasants, who comprise about 80 per cent of the population of the Soviet Union, still rankle under collectivization. One of the largely untold stories of the last war (now documented by captured Nazi films) is that of the cordial welcome the people of the Ukraine, the breadbasket of Europe, gave to their Nazi conquerors. As a matter of fact, the welcome extended to the Germans was not confined to the Ukraine but was displayed in all the occupied areas. What might have happened if the Nazis had cashed in on this asset, no one knows, but instead they unleashed a terror that equaled the Kremlin's, thus turning would-be friends into foes.

Moreover, countless Russians have reason for personal antagonism to the regime. Between ten and fifteen million men and women are held in slave-labor camps. To have at least 5 per cent of the population behind barbed wire is not a healthy situation—even in a dictatorship. Consider what your own emotions would be toward a government whose secret police dragged off a member of your family, or someone else dear to you, to an address always unknown.

All Soviet peoples live in virtual enslavement. The ordinary citizen is tied to his job, unable to move from place to place, constantly in fear of drawing upon himself the suspicion of the secret police. Among scholars and scientists the terror dulls the creative faculties and stifles initiative. Factory managers fear to try new methods lest a mistake mean a one-way ticket to Siberia. Even among the top-drawer elite, fear is paralyzing, for few have forgotten the great purge of the forty thousand in 1936–38, when a substantial percentage of the high command of the Red Army was liquidated and many of Stalin's own colleagues disappeared.

It is always difficult for a dictator to bequeath his power to a successor when there is no regular method or machinery to govern the succession. The beneficiary chosen is certain to be unacceptable to the other lieutenants. This is particularly true in the case of Russia, where Stalin first usurped power and then concentrated it into his own hands until his dictatorship has become an absolute despotism. Neither the Constitution of the USSR, nor the statutes of the Communist party nor the dogma of Marxism provides for the might that is Stalin's. Stalin has gone against one of the fundamental Communist principles—the idea of collective rule—in elevating himself to this pinnacle. He has relegated the Central Committee of the Communist party to a rather negligible position, and at the same time deified and glorified himself to the point where the Russian people are expected to reject, as sacrilege, the thought of a successor.

Presumably Stalin, well aware of all this, is seeking a return to the Constitution by proposing that, after his death, power be divided among his lieutenants. The difficulty is that absolute power, such as Stalin's, is indivisible. You cannot have a 33⅓ per cent dictator pulling in harness with two other 33⅓ per cent dictators. Sooner or later, and mostly sooner, one, two, or all three of the triumvirate will decide that the best interests of the proletariat can be served only if he assumes complete authority. That is where the shooting starts—with the strong probability that the military will be on one side and the secret police on the other.

Stalin's death is, of course, only one among several possibilities that might provoke strife, turbulence, civil commotion and other upheavals inside the Soviet Union.

John Foster Dulles holds that, moreover, there is an underlying conflict between the national aspirations of the great mass under Soviet sway and the ambitions for world conquest of International Communism. He is certain that, in time, this conflict will be resolved in favor of nationalism, of Russians for Russia, of Poles for Poland, of Hungarians for Hungary. In the opinion of General MacArthur, who has displayed brilliant insight into the oriental turn of mind, Stalin's death may well be the event that will bring into the open this very real conflict.

The defection of another satellite such as Yugoslavia might have similar repercussions. Indeed, it can be categorically said that the Kremlin, with its need for blind obedience, is quite as frightened by the dissent and opposition of another Communist state such as Yugoslavia as by the natural antagonism of a capitalist country such as the United States. For Soviet propaganda has succeeded only too well in portraying the United States as a nation of warmongers duped and exploited by Wall Street. But it is an altogether different story when a Tito, once glorified as hero and white hope of International Communism, has to be vilified overnight as a traitor and Fascist stool pigeon. Uprisings in the Ukraine and elsewhere could also fissure the Soviet monolith. And I am convinced that the present defections from Communist party ranks in Italy, one of the Kremlin's great hopes, as well as other defections pending elsewhere, are troubling Stalin very much indeed.

Speaking personally, I am pinning particular hope for the downfall of the Kremlin on the will of peoples to rule themselves. This striving is an underlying force in world history. Within the past few years we have seen this yearning toward independence surge to success in India and Indonesia, for example, despite the comparatively benign and beneficent reign of Great Britain and the Netherlands. I saw in Korea a people who, despite the fact that they had been totally dominated by the Japanese for fifty years, had retained a passion to govern themselves. The Poles won their independence after World War I because their fierce desire to rule themselves after 146 years of subjugation was still unquenched. I expect to see them win freedom back again, and I expect the Czechs to do likewise. It is this aspiration which is a very potent threat to the Kremlin. It may determine the character of any new regime which takes over and may thus reverse altogether the current direction of Soviet foreign policy.

If any of these things should happen, there is the chance that we may see emerging in the Kremlin a leadership which, out of necessity, would pull in its horns,

relax tyranny within, abstain from aggression and be-
have with at least some rudiments of decency in its
relations to other peoples. This condition would promise
the free world a reasonably secure coexistence. The best
thing that could happen would be a revolution inside
the USSR that would turn it toward democracy and
thus provide a solid basis for enduring peace.

In view of these possibilities we must keep in mind
our twofold purpose in waging the peace along all four
fronts. In the first place, we strengthen ourselves in
every way, in armor, in alliances and in vision. In the
second place, in the very process of waging the peace,
we help to hasten events which may either force the
present leadership to withdraw behind the Iron Curtain or perhaps even to be overthrown.

In proposing this program for waging the peace, I am
aware—as a businessman first and foremost—that it will
hardly help to reduce our taxes or balance our budget
immediately. Yet only the advent of a durable peace,
as against continuing outlays for a "cold war" or a general war, would cut our defense costs by enough billions
to make possible both a reduction in taxes and a concur-
rent balancing of the budget. Only thus can we expect
to reduce taxes and balance our budget.

Everyone knows the benefits of lowering taxes, but
to many the significance of a balanced budget is obscure.
Yet as one who has observed the workings of govern-

ments the world over, I should like to underscore the point that a government which lives beyond its means for too long a period brings to its people distress at all times and disaster sometimes. Only a government which lives within its means can ensure that financial stability which is the bedrock upon which a vital and expanding economy can be built.

All this, of course, is at the prosaic level of government finance, of material soundness and solvency. At the level of moral soundness and solvency, the advent of a durable peace would be the most momentous and inspiring event of the twentieth century. It would mean that for the first time in thirty-seven years the shadow of war or impending war would be lifted. It would mean that the billions which now finance the fantastic wastes of war or go into defense preparations could be diverted to constructive purposes. A single billion out of the fifty billion we will necessarily have to spend for bullets could finance some two hundred thousand one-year scholarships at our leading colleges and universities. And there would be four hundred million dollars left to finance slum-clearance projects in New York, Chicago, Memphis and Los Angeles, and another one hundred million dollars for atomic research to release this miraculous energy for the pursuits of peace.

Despite all current strains and anxieties, we are living in one of history's most privileged periods.

CONCLUSION

During the decade ahead of us, we must be willing to strive and sweat and sacrifice enough to wage the peace with high skill and consecration. Our purpose must be not only to redeem the promise of freedom for our children and our children's children but also for those of peoples held in bondage by the Soviet Union. This is the challenge, and this the reward for the bold hard tasks which confront us in our pilgrimage toward peace. We have now the opportunity to convert this mid-point of the twentieth century into the great turning point of all time. Only if we heed this opportunity and take hold of it with faith in ourselves can we keep faith with mankind. Only thus can we hope to find, when this decade of decision ends, that we have shaped the beginnings of the first durable peace that men have ever built.

Index